CELEBRATE YOUR ADOLESCENCE

A ROAD MAP FOR ADOLESCENTS FOR EDUCATING THEM TO EXPERIMENT & ADVENTURE, TO EXPLORE & ACCOMPLISH, AND TO EMERGE AS SELF-CONFIDENT, HEALTHY & RESPONSIBLE CITIZENS.

DR.A.VIJAYALAKSHMI

Made with ♥ on the Notion Press Platform
www.notionpress.com

To all the people who are committed to building the physical, psychological, emotional, social, sexual, and spiritual health of adolescents and helping and supporting them to evolve as responsible and productive assets of the Nation.

Contents

Foreword

M.M.Pallam Raju

Minister of State for Defence, Government of India

FOREWORD

I am happy to know that Dr. Aluri Vijaya Lakshmi, a reputed gynaecologist and doctor, and Managing Trustee, Centre for Empowerment and Development of Women, Kakinada has written a book on "Adolescents' Health."

I have gone through the book and feel that it would help in removing many misconceptions and disseminate authentic information to adolescents and also to parents and educators.

Adolescence is an age of transition between childhood and adulthood. It is the period when children rapidly change biologically, psychologically and socially.

Adolescent years are complex. Most adolescents navigate through the turbulent course from childhood to adulthood to become healthy individuals and productive citizens. But many fail due to circumstances beyond their control and lack of proper support system.

We need to understand and gain deeper insight into the complexities of child and adolescent minds. There are many misconceptions amongst growing children about functions of the human body and the various changes that occur during the growing period. It is necessary to provide them with authentic information and create awareness among the youth, especially the girls. I strongly believe that adolescent health issues should be incorporated in school curriculum.

I am confident that this book by Dr. Aluri Vijaya Lakshmi will be an excellent source of information on adolescent health and achieve its noble objective of creating awareness of health knowledge among the adolescents and thereby helping them to grow into effective and healthy adults.

(M.M. Pallam Raju)

Date: 7th August, 2012

Office: 108-B, South Block, New Delhi - 110011, Ph : 23792128, 23794621, Fax : 23016255, E-mail : rrm@nic.in

Prologue

PROLOGUE

Dr Shruti's mind is in turmoil. No matter how much she wanted to divert, her mind kept on going back to Anita again and again.

"What happened Anita?" Dr Shruti asked Anita gently. Hiding behind her mother with shy looks, Anita came close to Shruti. When Shruti repeated her question after waiting for a while, Anita burst into tears instead of speaking out.

"Why is she crying Santi?" Then Shruthi asked Anita's mother, who was also in tears.

"Mam! A lump started developing on her chest about 2 months back. She heard a health talk on breast cancer on TV some time ago. She thought that the lump on her chest was cancer. She was too worried and stopped eating and couldn't sleep. She was afraid to tell me. She revealed it only yesterday when the pain was bothering her. My whole family is trembling with fear since yesterday Madam!" told Santi, wiping her eyes.

"Don't worry. I will examine her. All lumps are not cancerous" Shruti tried to console them and asked the nurse to take the girl to the examination room.

"This lump is not cancer, but just a breast swelling, that appears naturally at puberty when the child is growing. Sometimes one breast develops earlier and the other breast starts growing later. That's why only Anita's right breast is growing. It is normal for some people to have mild pain in the breast swelling or breast bud at this stage." said Shruti after she examined Anita.

Anita and Santi sighed with relief, profusely thanked Shruthi and rushed to go home to announce the good news to the family members. Anitha, who was burning with fear and stopped, eating properly, felt extremely hungry now.

Dr Shruthi is deeply immersed in her thoughts. The problems with which the adolescent children came to her for medical advice and the tragic incidents that are happening day in and day out in the families and society, agitated her.

Shruti's mind revolved around a series of memories. Her mind wobbled with the recollection of the girl who got panicked with the onset of her 1st period, a girl who was a victim of sexual assault by a family member and committed suicide,and many more.

She is aware that millions of boys and girls do not have basic knowledge about the structure and functions of their bodies, the natural processes and the biological, psychological, emotional, sexual and social changes that take place in their bodies and minds.

They have no knowledge about how these changes impact negatively in terms of their health, education, development, growth, happiness etc., preventing them to groom as productive and responsible citizens.

She is also aware that the problems erupting in the lives of adolescents who do not have basic knowledge about their reproductive and sexual health, are creating chaos in their families and society.

This awareness and the agony she felt after knowing the real life incidents happening in adolescents lives,, had pushed Shruthi into deep introspection and reminded her of the responsibility of a healthcare provider to educate the adolescents and thus promote Adolescents' health.

Shruthi has decided to plan and implement a structure to create awareness among school-going and drop-out adolescents, especially those children who belong to communities that have been deprived of education and knowledge for centuries.

As a part of implementing the project, Dr Shruti came to conduct a health awareness program in a high school in the fishing area of the District. The Head Master and the teachers welcomed her and led her to the hall where the students have assembled.

From then on Dr Shruti conducted health education sessions in many schools and colleges. She addressed different dimensions and issues of adolescence and interacted with the children.

She encouraged them to express their doubts, challenges and concerns and tried to clarify them.

With that vast experience at the ground level, she wrote a series of books on “Adolescents’ Health and Behaviour.”

Here is the 1st one in the series.

"Celebrate Your Adolescence"

Read these books to transform as healthy adults

Acknowledgements

I profusely thank all the adolescent girls who had attended my sessions on Adolescents‘ health and shared their concerns, fears, doubts and experiences.

I also thank the teachers who had participated in the trainers’ training programs and pledged to educate the adolescent girls in their schools.

I am immensely happy to express my profound gratitude to the parents who are keen on Protecting their Adolescents Children' health and encouraged their children to attend my awareness programs

I am grateful to all the peoplewho have helped me in publishing the book, Mr.Sailu, Mr.Ravi.L.Tiwari and specially to my mentor , Mr.Som Batla who had guided me to self publish my book

Preface

Dr Shruti's mind is in turmoil. No matter how much she wanted to divert, her mind kept on going back to Anita again and again.

"What happened?" Dr Shruti asked Anita gently.

Hiding behind her mother with shy looks, Anita came close to Shruti. When Shruti repeated her question after waiting for a while, Anita burst into tears instead of speaking out.

"Why is she crying?" Then Shruthi asked Anita's mother, who was also in tears.

"Mam! A lump started developing on her chest about 2 months back. She heard a health talk on breast cancer on TV some time ago.

She thought that the lump on her chest was cancer. She was too worried and stopped eating and couldn't sleep. She was afraid to tell me. She revealed it only yesterday when the pain was bothering her. My whole family is trembling with fear since yesterday Madam!" told Santi, wiping her eyes

"Don't worry. I will examine her. All lumps are not cancerous" Shruti tried to console them and asked the nurse to take the girl to the examination room.

"This lump is not cancer, but just a breast swelling, that appears naturally at puberty when the child is growing. Sometimes one breast develops earlier and the other breast starts growing later. That's why only Anita's right breast is growing. It is normal for some people to have mild pain in the breast swelling or breast bud at this stage." said Shruti after she examined Anita.

Anita and Santi sighed with relief, profusely thanked Shruthi and rushed to go home to announce the good news to the family members. Anitha, who was burning with fear and stopped, eating properly, felt extremely hungry now.

Dr Shruthi is deeply immersed in her thoughts. The problems with which the adolescents came to her for medical advice and the tragic incidents that are happening day in and day out in the families and society, agitated her.

Shruti's mind revolved around a series of memories. Her mind wobbled with the recollection of the girl who got panicked with the onset of her 1st period, a girl who was a victim of sexual assault by her family member and committed suicide, and many more.

She is aware that millions of boys and girls do not have basic knowledge about the structure and functions of their bodies, the natural processes and the biological, psychological, emotional, sexual and social changes that take place in their bodies and minds.

They do not know how these changes impact negatively in terms of their health, education, development, growth, happiness etc., preventing them to groom as productive and responsible citizens.

She is also aware that the problems erupting in the lives of adolescents who do not have basic knowledge about their reproductive and sexual health are creating chaos in their families and society.

This recognition and the agony she felt after knowing the real-life incidents happening in Adolescents' lives had propelled Shruthi into soul searching and reminded her of the responsibility of a healthcare provider to educate the adolescents and thus promote Adolescents' health.

Shruthi has decided to plan and implement a structure to create awareness among school-going and out-of-school adolescents, especially those children who belong to communities that have been deprived of education and knowledge for centuries.

As a part of implementing the project, Dr Shruti came to conduct a health awareness program in a high school in the fishing area of the District. The Head Master and the teachers welcomed her and led her to the hall where the students have assembled.

From then on Dr Shruti conducted health education sessions in many schools and colleges. She addressed different dimensions and issues of adolescence and interacted with the children.

She encouraged them to express their doubts, challenges and concerns and tried to clarify them. With that vast experience at the ground level, she wrote a series of books on "Adolescents' Health and Behaviour"

Here is the 1st book in the series.

"Celebrate Your Adolescence"

Read this book to transform as healthy adults.

Why Should You Read This Book?

Did you ever questioned yourself:

- Am I Normal?
- Am I a child or an adult?
- Have you ever wondered why there are changes in your body?
- Did the changes make you feel embarrassed, scared or ashamed?
- Were you ever overwhelmed while experiencing the physical, psychological, emotional, sexual and social changes, all simultaneously?
- Rapid growth. . .Cause of Concern!
- Do you want to have a smooth, safe, healthy, happy and productive adolescence?

Then this book, **"Celebrate your Adolescence"** is for you.

Do you want to support your adolescent child to pass through this crucial phase of transition without the impact of myths, misconceptions and misinformation that lead to life-long consequences?

Do you want to guide your student to travel through the right path to attain holistic development through knowledge and achieve their full potential to emerge as productive and responsible citizens?

Here is a book,

A **torch** to throw light on the various challenges and opportunities adolescents encounter in this crucial phase of their lives.

A **resource** to provide authentic knowledge for Adolescents, enabling them to make well- informed choices.

A **tool** which helps to build systems and processes to strengthen and promote the positive health of adolescents.

This book gives you clear insights of Adolescence:

- The uniqueness of Adolescence and its different stages.
- What are the health challenges faced by adolescents in the fast-changing modern world?
- Barriers to achieving Adolescents' health
- Why adolescence is considered a problem age?
- Developmental tasks of Adolescents.
- Factors impacting the health of Adolescents

Puberty

- Puberty, its physiological aspects and the factors affecting the onset of puberty
- Age of onset of puberty and factors affecting the onset of puberty
- Factors impacting the early age of menarche
- Prepubescent phase, pubescent phase and post pubescent phase
- Primary and secondary sexual characteristics
- Physical changes in girls and boys during puberty

Disorders of puberty:
The normal process of puberty
Types of puberty disorders

- Precocious puberty
- Delayed puberty
- Contra-sexual pubertal development
    - Females-Virilization
    - Males-Feminization
- Premature Thelarche and Adrenarche

Puberty and adolescence-Hormonal changes

- How does the body know to grow?

- What happens on the inside that makes us change on the outside?
- Different hormones involved in pubertal changes and their functions: GNRH, FSH, LH, Prolactin, Estradiol, Progesterone, Testosterone

Nutrition in Adolescence

- Importance of good nutrition on the growth and development of adolescents.
- Why do adolescents require more nutrients?
- What is a balanced diet?
- Eating disorders and the hazards caused by bad eating habits
- Importance of having healthy eating habits.

Hygiene

Highlights the importance of regular hygienic practices, personal hygiene, cleanliness of living spaces, and surroundings, and clean water and food for the good health of adolescents, their families and communities

Fitness and Exercise

- Gives a picture of How regular Exercise helps..
- Maintaining a healthy weight and preventing obesity which poses many negative consequences,
- Gives energy and builds stamina
- Keeps adolescents fit.
- Boosts their immune systems and helps to stay healthy.

Promotes good sleep, which helps to maintain a positive mood.

- Acts as a mood booster by releasing hormones into the brain, which makes adolescents happier and ease the effects of depression, anxiety and ADHD.
- Prevention of heart ailments and diabetes and increasing good

cholesterol.

- Health hazards of a sedentary lifestyle.
- A structured plan to have a regular exercise schedule.

Addressing The Need...

About 1.3 billion, the largest generation of adolescents in history are transforming to enter adulthood in a rapidly changing world.

Adolescents are our assets and are a great potential resource for the future with fresh energy, ideas, and hope. During these years they are learning, exploring, and making decisions that affect the rest of their lives.

Adolescents are not a homogenous group. They have different needs depending on many factors, including gender, age, cognitive developmental stage, sexual activity, school status, familial relationships, and cultural norms.

Sexual activities of adolescents start before acquiring knowledge and skills in self-protection.

Many factors lead to early adolescent sexual activity outside of marriage, for eg. Reduced age of menarche and increased age of marriage, changing sexual norms, economic pressures, weakening social controls, absence of multigenerational extended family, absence of one or both parents, pressure on young people to be sexually active, mass media and social media influence, etc.

Adolescents are more at risk because of less access to reproductive and sexual health information that can help them make responsible decisions about their sexual behavior, health services being rarely designed specifically to address their needs, low levels of health-seeking behavior of adolescents, and legislation and policies which prevent sex education.

Without the appropriate information and services they need, adolescents are more likely to engage in high-risk behavior that can have adverse consequences like unintended and too-early pregnancies, and sexually transmitted diseases, Including HIV/AIDS and unsafe abortions.

Socio-cultural, political, and economic forces, such as poverty, migration, war, and civil disturbances increase the vulnerability of adolescents in developing countries.

Adolescents do not act simply as independent decision-makers but within the context of social and cultural influences. Therefore they need life skills programs to acquire skills to protect themselves from peer or adult coercion.

They should also reinforce group values against unsafe sexual behavior, both among peers and the community. Parents are often reluctant to talk about sexuality with their children out of embarrassment, lack of accurate information, or fear that they will appear to condone adolescent sexual activity.

Teachers suffer the same shortcomings as parents and require training and support to play their role effectively. Youth often cite peers and media as their primary sources of information.

Unfortunately, these sources are often filled with erroneous information and myths. Recognizing this fact, Young people wish they could get authentic information from well-informed sources.

The **"Adolescents' Health and Behaviour"** series is written to address this need, with a firm belief that Adolescents have a fundamental right to access accurate and comprehensive reproductive and sexual health information along with information about good nutrition, hygiene, fitness and exercise, mental health, life skills etc.

CHAPTER ONE

Know Your Adolescence

Shruti started the health education session by posing some questions to the students, enlightening them and addressing their doubts and concerns.

"Health is not a commodity that can be purchased. It is an asset which has to be assiduously maintained with care by following rules of conduct regarding diet, exercise and behaviour. Diseases occur in those who do not follow the rules of healthy living. The aim of medicine is threefold, promotion of positive health, prevention of disease and treatment of disease."

- *AYURVEDA*

The above three aims are more important today than in the past.

What is health?

WHO defines Health as not the mere absence of disease or deformity, but complete physical, mental, emotional, sexual, social and spiritual well-being.

Who is an adolescent?

Adolescent-No more a child, not yet an adult Adolescents – defined by the United Nations as those between the ages of 10 and 19.

The term adolescence is derived from the Latin term "Adolescere", which means "to grow up", or "to grow into maturity".

The traditional definition of adolescence is **"The period of life beginning with the appearance of secondary sex characteristics and ending with the cessation of somatic growth."**

With the advances of Physical and behavioural sciences relating to growth and development, adolescence is now defined by W.H.O. as a **Physico-psycho-social progress starting from age 10 to 20 years of age.**

Adolescence may be defined as that period within the life span when most of a person's characteristics are **changing from what is typically considered childlike to what is typically considered adult** like and refers to the transition period when psychological and social changes take place in a boy or girl.

Why is adolescence unique?

- Humans undergo different stages in their life and each and every stage of human development that happens from conception to death is marked by distinct and unique characteristics.
- Adolescence is a unique stage of human development and an important time for laying the foundations of good health.
- Adolescence begins at about 10 years in girls and for boys 2 years later, by the age of 12 years.
- The end of adolescence is not clearly delineated and varies with the physical, emotional, mental, social or cultural criteria that define the adult.
- For both boys and girls, there is wide individual variability in the time of onset and rate of adolescent changes. All the factors that contribute to this variability are not known. Some are definitely genetic, some are nutritional and some others are socio-economic.
- Adolescence is a crucial link between childhood and adulthood. Rapid Physical, cognitive, psychological, social, emotional, moral, educational and vocational development occurs during the stage of adolescence.
- This impacts how they feel, think, make decisions, and interact with the world around them and a complete metamorphosis of the individual takes place.
- Adolescence is the stage of development that is marked by the onset of puberty in the beginning and the attainment of

physiological and psychological maturity at the end.

- Adolescence is the critical process allowing the individual to leave childhood dependence and enter dramatic changes that finalize in autonomous adulthood.
- The body develops in size, strength and reproductive capabilities.
- The mind becomes capable of more abstract thinking, future orientation and ethical convictions.
- Social relationships move from a family sphere to a wider horizon in which other adults and peers come to play significant roles.
- All these changes are interrelated, Development is usually uneven, and varies from individual to individual.
- The adolescent is childlike in some spheres and continues to need strong material and psychosocial support in others.
- The increase in sex steroid production will ensure the appearance and maintenance of sexual characteristics and the capacity for reproduction. The entire endocrine system is altered during adolescence.
- During this phase, adolescents establish patterns of behaviour – for instance, related to diet, physical activity, substance use, and sexual activity – that can affect their health positively or put their health at risk now and in the future.
- Adolescence is a transition period which may involve new risks but may present tremendous opportunities to influence positively the immediate and future health of adolescents.
- Adolescence is a critical time of identity formation, with the outset of puberty comes an explosion of growth-physical, intellectual, emotional, social, and spiritual.
- It is a period of preparation for undertaking greater responsibilities like familial, social, cultural and economic issues in adulthood.
- Adolescents have specific needs which vary with gender, life circumstances and socio-economic conditions.

- Though Adolescence is considered to be a healthy stage of life, there is significant death, illness and injury in the adolescent years, which is mostly preventable or treatable.
- Young and growing children have poor knowledge and lack of awareness about physical and psychological changes that occur during adolescence and the ill health affecting them.
- But it is important to encourage the adolescent to experiment, adventure, explore and accomplish.
- Understanding the nature and scope of adolescent development and responding appropriately, requires patience, and empathy, and is very crucial for their holistic development.

Adolescents are the future of the nation, Major Demographic & economic force.

Adolescents are the greatest resource for a society to thrive.

Investments in adolescents bring a triple benefit:

- Healthy Adolescents Now,
- Healthy Adults in the future,
- Healthy future generations.

Why is Adolescents' health a Low priority in Public health programs?

Adolescents are among the healthiest people in all societies in terms of morbidity and mortality.They have survived diseases of infancy and childhood health risks which still contribute to high mortality and morbidity taking a huge toll, and they are not yet suffering from the disabilities of old age or from damage arising from decades of hard labour and stress at home and at the workplace.

That is why the health of adolescents has traditionally received low priority in public health programs.

What is the reason for the growing interested in adolescent health in recent times global

Adolescents' heath has gained much attention globally because of the increasing awareness that the habits, attitudes and behaviour developed during these formative years, will impact the rest of their adult lives.

More than 1.2 billion adolescents between the age group of 10-19 years, largest in the known history, make up 16 per cent of the world's population and are ready to take up the role of agents of development. Thus,

- The youth of any country are crucial to its development. It is important to note that their impressionable minds can be moulded very easily.
- When compared to other stages of human life, physical illness is much less in the adolescent age group.
- A large number of problems adolescents face are due to their **risk-taking behaviours** which can easily be **prevented by appropriate information, education, preventive counselling and anticipatory guidance** to reduce the high-risk behaviour and its consequences.
- The health impact of a growing number of adolescent pregnancies contributes to high maternal mortality, Infant Mortality and low birth weight babies, and high incidence of sexually transmitted diseases including HIV and nutritional deficiency disorders, especially anaemia in adolescents (70% in girls) are matters of concern.
- An adolescent requires adequate physical, mental and emotional nourishment to develop and blossom into a healthy, strong and productive young adult.
- Building developmental assets and value education in the adolescent phase is very crucial. **Parents, teachers and peers play an important role** in achieving this goal.
- Truly successful people live with high ethics and good morals. Adolescents need guidance in identifying what are **"Good**

Morals and Good ethics"

- The word **'Moral'** conveys all aspects of a person- thoughts, feelings and behaviour guided by the highest standards by which we lead our lives.
- **'Ethics'** means principles and standards of human conduct which govern an individual, society and nation. The ethical concerns of adolescents are the same world over.

Adolescents' health problems-What are the categories?

The health problems of adolescents fall broadly into two categories:

- Those, over which they have little or no control, especially those which originate in childhood.
- Those which are largely the result of their behaviour which again is the product of many factors.

What are the factors impacting the health of adolescents?

People and conditions in the:

- Family
- School
- Community
- Places of recreation, work and worship
- The mass media
- The social media
- Health sectors

What are the Health challenges faced by adolescents?

- Injuries
- Mental health
- Adolescent pregnancy
- HIV/AIDS
- Violence

- Alcohol & drugs
- Nutrition
- Malnutrition and obesity
- Exercise
- Infectious disease

What are the barriers for Adolescents' health?

Major barriers

- Access and availability of health care services are very much limited for adolescents.
- Lack of accurate information.
- Absence of proper guidance.
- Parents' ignorance.
- Lack of skills.
- Insufficient services from health care delivery system.
- Poor quality of clinical services.

Unwelcoming.

High cost.

- Gender barriers.
- Peer pressure.
- Fear of disclosure.
- Poverty.
- Legal or cultural restrictions.
- Unsafe environments etc.

What are the markers of end of Adolescence?

- Physical and sexual maturation,
- Social and financial freedom,
- Development of self- identity,
- Acquisition of capabilities needed to fulfil the adult relationships and roles

- The capacity for abstract thinking and reasoning.

Why adolescence is considered as a problem age?

- Many adolescents are inexperienced and are not capable to cope up with problems all alone, as their problems are solved in parts by parents and teachers so far. Thus they easily get frustrated if something goes wrong.
- Parents expect them to behave as mature people, but consider them immature while entrusting them any responsibility. This dual attitude irritates them.
- Adolescents feel that they are independent and are capable of handling their problems and they demand for the right of
- Coping with their own problems.
- Adolescents easily get influenced by peer group.
- This is the age of curiosity especially towards substances, drugs and sex.

What are the Developmental Tasks of Adolescence?

- Adolescence is not merely related to age alone that signifies the beginning or end of it. Adolescence is related to the achievement of important developmental milestones.
- Achieving new and more mature relations with same age people of both sexes.
- Achieving a masculine or feminine social role.
- Accepting one's physique and using the body effectively.
- Achieving emotional independence from parents and other adults.
- Preparing for marriage and family life.
- Preparing for an economic career.
- Acquiring a set of values and an ethical system as a guide to behaviour; developing an ideology.
- Desiring and achieving socially responsible behaviour.

Stages of Adolescent Development

#A) Early Adolescence-Approximately 10-14 years of age

Physical changes:

Both girls and boys:

- Gains in height and weight,
- Growth of pubic/underarm hair
- Increased perspiration Increased oil production of hair and skin

Girls:

◦ Breast development and MenstruationBoys:

Boys

- Growth of testicles and penis
- Nocturnal emissions(Wet dreams)
- Deepening of voice
- Facial hair

Psychological changes:

- Identity Development and Movement towards independence:
    - Emerging identity shaped by in/external influences
    - Moodiness
    - Improved speech to express oneself
    - More likely to express feelings by action than by words, (may be more true for males)
    - Close friendships importance
    - Less attention shown to parents, with occasional rudeness and realization that parents are not perfect
    - Identification of own faults.
    - Search for new people to love in addition to parents.

  - Tendency to return to childish behaviour during times of stress.
  - Peer group influence on personal interests and clothing styles.

- Future interests and cognitive development
- Increasing career interests, mostly interested in present and near future.
- Greater ability to work.

Sexuality

- Girls mature faster than boys
- Shyness, Blushing, and modesty.
- More showing off.
- Greater interest in privacy.
- Experimentation with body (masturbation).
- Worries about being normal.
- Self-exploration and evaluation.

Peer group

- Important for their development
- Intense friendships with same sex
- Contact with opposite sex in groups

#B) Middle Adolescence-14-17 years
Physical changes

- Males show continued height and weight gain, while female growth slows down (females grow only 1-2 inches after their first menstrual period).
- Reach approximately 95% of adult growth.
- **Psychological changes:**
- Identity development and movement toward independence.

Self -involvement

- Alienating between unrealistically high expectations and worries about failure
- Complaints that parents interfere with independence
- Extremely concerned with appearance and body
- Lowered opinion of and withdrawal from parents
- Effort to make new friends
- Strong emphasis on the new peer group
- Periods of sadness as the psychological loss of parents takes place
- Examination of inner experiences which may include writing a dairy.

Future interests and Cognitive development

- Intellectual interests gain importance
- Some sexual and aggressive energies directed into creative and career interests
- Anxiety can emerge related to school and academic performance.

Ethics and self –direction

- Development of ideals and selection of role models
- More consistent evidence of conscience
- Greater goal setting capacity
- Interest in moral reasoning

Peer Groups

- Strong peer friendships

- Peer group most important and determines behaviour.

Sexuality

- Concerns about sexual attractiveness
- Frequently changing relationships
- More clearly defined sexual orientation, with internal conflict often experienced by those who are not heterosexual
- Tenderness and fears shown towards opposite sex
- Feelings of love and passion
- Forms stable relationships

#C) Late Adolescence-16-19 year's
Physical changes

- Most young women are fully developed, young men continue to gain weight, muscle mass, body hair.
- Identity development and movement towards independence
- Firmer identity
- Ability to think through ideas
- Ability to express ideas in words
- More developed sense of humour
- Interests and emotions become more stable
- Ability to make independent decisions
- Ability to compromise
- Pride in one's work
- Self-reliance
- Greater concern for others

Future interests and cognitive development

- More defined work habits.
- Higher level of concern for the future.
- Thoughts about one's role in life.

Ethics and self-direction

- Useful insight
- Focus on personal dignity and self -esteem
- Ability to set goals and follow through
- Acceptance of social institutions and cultural traditions.

Self -regulation of self-esteem.

- **Peer groups**
    - Decisions/values less influenced by peers in favour of individual friendships.
    - Selection of partner based on individual choice rather than what others think.
- **Sexuality**
    - Concerned with serious relationships.
    - Clear sexual identity.
    - Capacities for tender and sensuous love.
    - Mutual and balanced sexual relations.

Facts about Adolescents in developing countries

- 22%of the Population is adolescents and Girls make up 47% of Adolescents.
- In India, adolescents comprise a sizeable population - there are 243 million adolescents comprising nearly one-fifth of the total population (21.4%).
- Composition varies by age and sex - Of the total population, 12.1% belong to 10-14 age group and 9.7 % are in the 15-19 age group. Female adolescents comprise 46.9% and male adolescents 53.1 % of the total population.
- Anaemia and stunting are widely prevalent, especially in girls.
- Findings from (NFHS 3) indicate that as many as 56% of females and 30% of males in the 15 - 19 age group are anaemic.

- In 15 - 19 yrs. age group 47% females and 58% males are thin and 2.4% females and 2% males suffer from obesity.
- At least 50% all young women are sexually active by age 18, mostly within marriage, as the incidence of child marriages is very high.
- 50% of girls are married by 18 age years, almost 20% are pregnant by age 15, with the inherent risks of 100% increase in maternal and infant mortality and morbidity.
- Maternal mortality rate due to teenage pregnancy is 9% (2007-2009) –Maternal mortality of teenage mothers is a grave cause for concern. TFR amongst 15-19 yrs. old is 14% in urban and 18% in rural of the total fertility
- At least 10 million unintended pregnancies occur each year among adolescent girls aged 15–19 years in the developing world.
- Of the estimated 5.6 million abortions that occur each year among adolescent girls aged 15–19 years, 3.9 million are unsafe, contributing to maternal mortality, morbidity and lasting health problems.
- Adolescent mothers (ages 10–19 years) face higher risks of eclampsia, puerperal endometritis, and systemic infections than women aged 20 to 24 years, and babies of adolescent mothers face higher risks of low birth weight, preterm delivery and severe neonatal conditions.
- Unmet need for contraceptives - The contraceptive knowledge is quite high among adolescents but there are high gaps between knowledge and usage. Only 23% of married girls reported use of any contraceptive method.
- Premarital sex relations are increasing.
- Trafficking and prostitution have increased - Extreme poverty, low status of women, lax border checks and the collision of law enforcement officials has led to increase in prostitution. Expansion of trafficking and clandestine movement of young girls has also increased across national and international borders.

- RTIs are common in young women. Misconceptions about HIV/AIDS are widespread. 32-42 % of people living with HIV/AIDS in India are between the ages of 15-29.
- There is a high level of awareness about HIV among young people especially among those who are more literate. As per (NFHS 3) awareness of STls' and HIV/AIDS was limited in 15-24 years age group. Just 19% of young men and 15% of young women reported awareness of STI.
- There are marked inequalities in education among adolescents in India. 53% dropout during class 1 - 10, only 2.35% adolescent continue higher secondary education with high dropout rate for both girls and boys.
- Child Labour: Economic compulsions force many to work - Nearly one out of three adolescents in 15-19 years is working - 20.6 % as main workers and 11.7 % as marginal workers. Economic compulsions force adolescents to participate in the workforce.
- Despite adult unemployment, employers like to engage children and adolescents because of cheap labour.
- 40% of adolescents start drugs &substance abuse between 15-20 year.

- Girls and rural adolescents are disadvantaged. Low status of women in the family and society, gender bias and gender violence are also impacting negatively on the reproductive and sexual health (RSH) of adolescent girls and women.
- Crimes against adolescents are prevalent - Both boys and girls are subjected to sexual abuse and are at risk for STIs/HIV/AIDS. Sexual abuse of both boys and girls cuts across economic and social classes. According to a survey, in 84 % cases, the victims knew the offenders and 32 % of the offenders were neighbours.
- Crimes against girls range from eve teasing to abduction, rape, prostitution and violence to sexual harassment. Unfortunately, social taboos prevent these crimes from being registered. Even when registered, prosecution rarely takes place.

- Sexual coercion (forcible sex) results in adolescent girls' risk to unwanted pregnancy.
- Adolescent girls lack the knowledge about the basics of the natural processes of puberty, menstruation, sexual and reproductive health, pregnancy and contraception.
- Information from Uninformed sources: Adolescents learn more about sexual and reproductive health from uninformed sources, which results in the perpetuation of myths and misconceptions about puberty, menstruation, pregnancy, childbirth etc.
- Social norms and cultural system prohibit talking about sex. As such, providing reproductive and sexual health information and services to adolescents in countries like India, is challenging. As a result, adolescents are shrouded in myths and misconceptions about sexuality.
- The special needs of adolescents are rarely addressed by the educational, health, and family welfare programs.
- More than 33% of the diseases burden and almost 60% of premature deaths among adults can be associated with behaviours or conditions that began or occurred during adolescence for eg. Tobacco, alcohol use, poor eating habits, sexual abuse and risky sex (WHO 2002).
- Habits and lifestyles of adolescents are responsible for 70% of premature.
- Adolescents need social skills that will enable them to say **"No"** to sex with confidence and to negotiate safer sex if they wish to.
- Adolescent girls must be able to decide consciously and freely whether, when, and with whom to become sexually active; to avoid non-consensual sex, sexual violence, and abuse; to plan pregnancies and to have access to safe abortion; to avoid acquiring or transmitting sexually transmitted infections and HIV/AIDS.

For this to happen:
Adolescents need information, including:

- AgeAppropriate, comprehensive sexuality education
- Opportunities to develop life skills.
- Health services that are acceptable, equitable, appropriate and effective.
- Need a safe and supportive environment in their families and communities to undergo these changes in safety, with confidence and with the best prospects to transform as healthy and productive adults.
- They also need opportunities to meaningfully and proactively participate in the design and delivery of interventions to improve and maintain their health.
- Expanding and ensuring such opportunities is crucial to responding to adolescents' specific needs and rights.

Adolescents need accurate & authentic information and skills
Adolescents need encouragement

Parents and other family members, teachers, peers and other people who can influence the adolescents have to be supportive and empathetic of the turmoil the adolescents go through to enable the smooth transition into adulthood.

It is also important that the opportunity for independent experiment, adventure and accomplishment be encouraged.

"Good Health & Wisdom" "Greatest Blessings!"

CHAPTER TWO

Puberty - Physical Growth & Sexual Development

"Before puberty, the child's personality has not yet formed and it is easier to guide its life and make it acquire specific habits of order, discipline, and work." - Antonio Gramsci

Puberty and adolescence are two terms interlinked with each other representing certain changes and periods of such changes.

The biological and physiological changes during the **"adolescent growth spurt"** involve almost all organs of the body.

During Puberty, somatic as well as skeletal growth is related to sexual development, as adolescent growth is initiated and controlled by sex hormones.

What is puberty?

From the day of birth, the child begins to grow up. As the child grows, their body, thoughts, and feelings change.

Sometime between the ages Of 9 to 16 years, a girl begins to change into a young woman and between the ages of 11 to 16 years, a boy begins to change into a young man.

They may have thoughts such as **"What is happening to me?"** or **"Is this normal?"**

This process of change is called **puberty.**

- Puberty refers to the physical changes leading to sexual maturity in a boy or a girl. It is the beginning of the transition from childhood to adulthood, the period when children rapidly change biologically, psychologically, socially, and cognitively.
- From a biological perspective, puberty is the stage of physical maturation, reproductive organs start maturing during puberty in which an individual becomes physiologically capable of sexual reproduction.
- The biological changes that occur during puberty include several hormones, all of which modulate somatic growth, the development of the sex glands, and their endocrine as well as exocrine secretions.
- Puberty is a sequence of events in which physical changes occur, resulting in adult physical characteristics and the capacity to reproduce.
- The physical changes are regulated by changes in the levels of hormones that are produced by the **pituitary gland- luteinizing hormone and follicle-stimulating hormone**.
- At birth levels of these hormones are high, but they decrease within a few months and remain low until puberty. Early in puberty, levels of luteinizing hormone and follicle-stimulating hormone increase, stimulating the production of sex hormones.
- The increased levels of sex hormones, primarily **estrogen**, result in physical changes in girls, including maturation of the breasts, ovaries, uterus, and vagina.
- The increased levels of the sex hormone, Testosterone result in physical changes in boys.

When does puberty happen?

Puberty begins at different ages in different individuals. Girls begin to show pubertal changes earlier (ages of 9 and 14, Average 10.5 years) than boys (10to17 Average 11.5 years).

The entire process can take anywhere from three to six years.

However, it is essentially the activation of the **Hypothalamic-pituitary-gonadal axis** that induces and enhances the progressive ovarian and testicular sex hormones secretion which is responsible for the profound biological, morphological, and psychological changes to which the adolescent is subjected

Factors affecting the onset of puberty:

When puberty begins and how quickly its changes occur are influenced by many other factors, such as Development during infancy and childhood.

Organic factors: Heredity, the nervous system, end organs and tissues, Adolescent's family, Society, culture, and environment.

Nutrition and general health:

The calorie requirement for adolescents is higher than that for adults who are engaged in physical labor or lactating mothers, as the adolescent period is a rapidly growing stage and the need for nutritious food is higher in this period.

Girls require more nutrition as they lose blood in their monthly periods.

The deleterious effects of malnutrition depend both on severity and chronicity.

Severe and chronic malnutrition causes permanent stunting.

In developed countries, puberty begins about 3 years earlier today than it did a century ago. The reasons probably include improvements in nutrition and general health.

Weight:

Puberty tends to start earlier in girls who are slightly overweight and tends to start later in girls who are greatly underweight and malnourished.

Genetics:

- Puberty occurs earlier in girls whose mothers matured early. The effect of genetic factors is far more evident. The familial genetic effect applies to skeletal maturation at all ages.
- Another indication of the role of genetic factors is the relationship between physique, which is constitutionally determined, and the age of menarche- girls who have a linear build mature later than girls who are short and stocky.

- However, it is not yet clear whether short stature precipitates early menarche or vice versa.
- Boys who are linear in build mature later than boys who are short and stocky

Ethnic group:

Puberty tends to start earlier in blacks and Hispanics than in Asians and whites who are not Hispanic.

Climate and Season:

- The season of the year has a well-documented effect on the velocity of growth: height increases as fast in the spring, and growth in weight is four to five times as fast in the autumn. During spring, there is a significant reduction in the incidence of menarche.
- But the physical mechanism responsible for the seasonality of the growth is unknown.

Disease and Illness:

- Retardation of growth depends on the severity, duration and nature of the illness, all chronic diseases, which restrict the child to bed for a prolonged period, cause retardation of growth temporarily and the growth catches up once the child becomes normal.
- The specific mechanism by which illness causes retardation of growth is not known clearly and probably varies with the nature of the disease. The neural and endocrine mechanisms regulating growth might get disrupted.

Socio-economic class:

Studies revealed a difference of about 2 inches in height between the **children of professionals and Managers** and those of **unskilled labourers** at puberty, mostly due to nutritional and health status and other benefits of a higher standard of living.

Emotional factors:

Psycho-social dwarfism is the result of emotional disturbances in early life. Stunting of growth is noticed in children with eating disorders and other reactions to emotional disturbances in the parents.

These children revert to normal when they are separated from the adverse environment.

The acceleration Trend:

- Acceleration of growth has been evident during the past century, menarche occurred earlier by 2-3 months per decade which has slowed down of late in some of the developed countries.

- Acceleration is also observed in height and weight, the reasons for which are unknown.

Early age of menarche- Factors impacting:

- Improved nutrition and higher standard of living
- Control of diseases in the growing period
- Better healthcare
- Changes in World climate and temperature and
- Environmental factors

All the above factors may have a role to do. **Physical growth during Adolescence.**

Physiology of growth

Growth involves an interaction between the body's endocrine and skeletal systems.

- Human Growth hormone, secreted by the pituitary, is the Key hormone for growth, which in turn, is regulated by Growth hormone releasing factor (GHRF) and somatisatin.

- The effects of growth hormone are modulated by Insulin-like growth factors (IGF1 and IGF 2 mainly). Human growth hormone stimulates IGF1, which affects bone growth.
- The maturation of bones is influenced by Thyroid hormones, adrenal androgens and gonadal sex steroids.
- The ending of the growth spurt is secondary to the closure of epiphysis, caused by sex steroids. Growth spurt.

Growth Spurts:
From Boys to Men:
Boys:

- The peak growth spurt for boys happens later than it does for girls.
- It occurs around six months after pubic hair development.
- When it does, the boy's shoulders will become fuller and broader, and they'll grow taller, too.
- Their face shape will look less round and more adult-like.
- Depending on when puberty starts, they may not reach their adult height until their late teens or even early 20s.

Height:

- Height velocity increases and peaks during an adolescent growth spurt.
- Growth in the adolescent stage accounts for 20% to 25% of the final adult height.
- The average growth spurt lasts two to 2-3 years.
- The growth spurt is variable from adolescent to adolescent.
- Growth during the peak height velocity for normal females is 5.4 cm. to 11.2 cm., in males, it is 5.8 cm. To 13.1 cm.

Weight:

- Weight velocity increases and reaches its peak during the adolescent growth spurt.
- The adolescent gains 50% of the Adult's body weight during adolescence.
- The onset of accelerated weight gain and the peak weight velocity is variable.
- The difference in growth spurts between males and females:
- PHV (Peak height velocity) occurs about 18-24 months earlier in females than in males.
- PHV in females averages 2 cm per year less than in males.
- PWV (Peak weight velocity) coincides with PHV in males, but PWV occurs 6-9 months after PHV in females Lean body mass.
- In females, the lean body mass increases in total amount, but decreases in percentage, because adipose mass increases at a greater rate.
- In males, the lean body mass increases and reflects increased muscle mass because of circulating androgens.

Adipose Mass:

- Body fat Increases in females and decreases in males during adolescence.

Skeletal Mass:

- Bone mass changes are parallel to the changes in lean body mass.
- The maturation of epiphyses occurs under the influence of estrogen in females and testosterone in males.

Pelvic remodeling in females:

- During puberty female pelvis widens more rapidly than the increase in anteroposterior diameter (from front to back).
- The forefront of the pelvis also widens and becomes rounder.

Internal organs:

- The growth of the brain, heart, liver, and kidneys during puberty is less than that of muscle and bone. Hence, the percentage of body weight represented by these organs decreases from 10% to 5%.
- Bodily changes affect height, weight, fat and muscle distribution, glandular secretions, and sexual characteristics.

Prepubescent phase:

- When some of these changes have begun, but most are yet to occur, the person is said to be in the prepubescent phase.
- The period of pre-pubescence begins with the first indication of sexual maturation. It ends with the initial appearance of pubic hair.

In males:

1. A continuing enlargement of the testicles.
2. An enlargement and reddening of the scrotal sac.
3. An increase in the length and circumference of the penis.

In females:

1.Prepubescent changes typically begin an average of two years earlier than in males.
2.The first phenomena of female development in this period are the enlargement of the ovaries and the ripening of the ova.
3.In contrast with those of males, these changes in primary sexual characteristics are not outwardly observable.
4.However, changes involving secondary sex characteristics can be seen (e.g., the rounding of the hips and the first phase of breast development).

5.The latter begins with an elevation of the areola surrounding the nipple, which produces a small cone-like growth called the breast bud.As with the male, there is no true pubic hair, although down may be present.

Pubescent phase:

When most of those bodily changes that will eventually take place have been initiated, the person is in the pubescent phase.

I. **In females**

- There is increased breast development, with the breast buds enlarging to form the primary breast.
- Another key change of pubescence in females is menarche, or the onset of menstruation, which occurs about 18 months after the maximum height increase of the growth spurt and typically is not accompanied initially by ovulation.
- The age of menarche, for example, varies among countries and even among different cultures within one country.
- Moreover, there has been a historical trend downward in the average age of menarche, translating into a decrease of several months per decade from about 1840 to the present. This phenomenon is generally ascribed to the improved health and nutrition of children and adolescents.

The vulva and clitoris enlarge.

II. **In males**

- The testes continue to enlarge, and the scrotum grows and becomes pigmented.
- The penis becomes longer and increases in circumference.
- The voice deepens.
- Pigmented axillary and facial hair appear, usually about two years after the emergence of pubic hair.

Post-pubescent phase:

- The phase of post-pubescence starts when pubic hair growth is complete.
- A deceleration of growth in height occurs.
- Changes in the primary and secondary sexual characteristics are essentially complete, and the person is fertile.
- Some changes in primary and secondary sexual characteristics occur in this phase, for instance, in males, it is during this period that the beard begins to grow; in females, there may be further breast development.
- This period ends when all bodily changes associated with adolescence are completed.

What are the Primary and secondary sexual characteristics?
Primary sexual characteristics:

- Primary sexual characteristics are those characteristics that are inborn and are present at birth while secondary sexual characteristics are those which emerge at puberty.
- Primary sexual characteristics comprise the external and internal genitalia.
- Male primary sexual characteristics are the penis and the scrotum, which allow a male to make and deliver sperm.
- Female primary sexual characteristics are the Vulva, clitoris, vagina, cervix, uterus, fallopian tubes, ovaries, and the ability to bear children.

Secondary sexual characteristics:

- Secondary sexual characteristics are the result of hormonal changes in the body during puberty.
- Testosterone, a hormone produced in the testis of males, and estrogens, produced in the ovaries of females are responsible for these changes in the males and females respectively.

- These changes are faster in girls than in boys. Some changes are common in both boys and girls while others are specific to each gender. This is due to the different hormones released by them.
- Growth of pubic hair, facial hair, and axillary hair, increase in height, sweating, etc. are some of the secondary sexual characteristics.
- Sweat and Sebaceous glands: The pimples and acne in adolescents are mostly due to the increased activities of sweat and sebaceous glands.

Male secondary sex characteristics:

- The first sign of puberty in boys is an increase in testicle size.
- About a year later, the penis and scrotum start to grow.
- Semen can be released during an erection when they are awake or when they are asleep.
- Growth of body hair, including underarm, abdominal, chest hair, and pubic hair.
- Growth of facial hair.
- Enlargement of the larynx (Adam's apple) and deepening of the voice.
- Increased stature; adult males are taller than adult females, on average.
- Heavier skull and bone structure.

The stages of genital maturity in **males** were graded as follows:
Stage 1:

- The testes, scrotum, and Penis are about the same size and proportion as in early childhood.

Stage 2:

- The scrotum and testes enlarge and the scrotal sac reddens and changes in texture.

- There is little or no enlargement of the penis.

Stage 3:

- There is further growth of the testes and scrotum.
- The penis begins to enlarge, mainly in length.

Stage 4:

- The testes and scrotum continue to enlarge and the scrotal skin continues to darken.
- The penis continues to grow in breadth and length with the development of the glans.

Stage 5:

- The genitalia is of adult size and shape. No further enlargement takes place.

Body hair:

- Body hair will start to grow and become thicker. For both boys and girls, new hair will start growing in the armpits and pubic area around the genitals.
- Arm and leg hair gets thicker. Boys also may start developing chest and facial hair.

The stages of Pubic hair in both boys and girls- grades:
Stage 1:

- The villus of the pubis resembles that of the abdomen.

Stage 2:

- Sparse growth of long, slightly pigmented, downy hair, straight or only slightly curled, appears chiefly at the base of the penis.

Stage 3:

- The hair is considerably darker, courser, and more curled. It spreads sparsely over the junction of the pubis.

Stage 4:

- The hair is now adult-like in coarseness and curliness, but the area covered is still considerably smaller than in most adults. There is no spread to the medial surface of the thighs.

Stage 5:

- The hair is adult in quantity and type, distributed in the "male" pattern of an inverse triangle, and may spread to the medial surface of the thighs.
- The onset of puberty in boys may be earlier than in the past and there are racial and ethnic differences.

Thus:

- Growth kinetics are augmented from early puberty, however, maximal velocity is attained only around 14 to 15 years of age.
- Progressively, the testis increases in size, mainly at the expense of the seminiferous tubules. The interstitial (Leydig) cells develop and ensure the synthesis and secretion of testosterone.
- A testicular volume of 4 ml or a longitudinal diameter greater than or equal to 2.5 cm and a slight progressive increase in scrotal folds and pigmentation constitute the first signs of puberty.
- Then the progression of pubertal development including penile size follows in close relation to the secretion of testosterone

(stage P3), followed by the growth of pubic hair several months later.

- Axillary hair appears around 13 years of age with characteristic body odor and lowering of the voice pitch, and acne is frequent.
- Finally, although prostatic development is initiated earlier, spermarche occurs at a mean age of 14 years.

Female Secondary Sexual Characteristics:
Changes in External & Internal Genital Organs:

- Secondary sexual development in girls involves the enlargement of the ovaries, uterus, vagina, labia, and breasts and the growth of pubic hair.
- The vagina, uterus, and fallopian tubes develop and grow in size under the influence of oestrogen. Glands in the vagina and cervix start to produce watery secretions under the influence of oestrogen.
- During puberty, ovaries increase in size and will start to produce two hormones – oestrogen and progesterone.
- In girls oestrogen hormone is responsible for the development of breasts, pubic hair, rounding of hips, and menstruation.
- The first sign is a growth spurt, though the first visible sign is Thelarche(Breast budding).
- The next sign is Pubarche i.e. appearance of pubic and axillary hair, followed by Peak height velocity, followed by the onset of menstruation.
- External genitals, The labia minora, and labia majora will often change in appearance during puberty. Everyone's genitals look different. The vulva may be different in shape, size, and colour.

Budding Breasts:

- Breast growth is usually the first sign of puberty that girls will notice. First, small lumps form behind the nipples. They can be sore, but the pain wanes away as breasts grow and change shape over the next few years.

- As they grow, it's not unusual for one breast to develop more slowly than the other, but they will even out in time.
- Boys also may have some swelling in their chest but it reduces within a year or two.

Breast stage 1 (B1):

- **Pre-pubertal:** no glandular tissue.
- **Areola and papillae**: areola conforms to general chest line.

Breast stage 2(B2)

- **Breasts:** Breast bud; Small amounts of glandular tissue.
- Areola: areola widens.

Breast stage 3(B3)

- **Breasts:** Larger and more elevation extends beyond the areolar parameter.
- **Areola and papilla:** Areola continues to enlarge but remains in contour with breast.

Breast stage 4(B4)

- **Breast:** Larger and more elevation.
- **Areola and Papillae**: form a mound projecting from the breast contour.

Breast stage 5(B5)

- **Breasts:** Adult (size variable)
- **Areola and Papillae**: Areola and breast are in the same plane, with papillae projecting above the areola.

In both sexes, these stages reflect the progressive modifications of the external genitalia and of sexual hair. Secondary sex characteristics appear at a mean age of 10.5 years in girls and 11.5 to 12 years in boys.

Other Changes developed in Boys:

- Boys develop heavier muscular bodies, wide shoulders, and narrow hips.
- Enlargement of the voice box leads to a much deeper voice.
- Maturation of the testis and starts to produce sperm.
- The growth of hairs on the chest.
- Enlargement of Adam's apple.

Other Changes developed in girls:

- Rounded hips and breast development. About a year after puberty begins, girls have a growth spurt.
- A girl will get taller and start to get wider hips and fuller breasts. Some curve-related fat will appear on their stomach, buttocks, and legs. Girls usually reach adult height by their mid-to-late teens. Matured ovaries start to release a mature ovum. Ovulation and menstruation initiate.
- Mammary gland enlargement

First signs of puberty in girls:

- The first sign of puberty in girls is usually that their breasts begin to develop.
- It's normal for breast buds to sometimes be very tender or for one breast to start to develop several months before the other one.
- Pubic hair also starts to grow, and some girls may notice more hair on their legs and arms.

Later signs of puberty in girls:

- After a year or so after the beginning of puberty, and for the next couple of years:
- Breasts continue to grow and become fuller.
- Around 2 years after beginning puberty, girls usually have their first period.
- Pubic hair becomes coarser and curlier.
- Underarm hair begins to grow – some girls also have hair in other parts of their body, such as their top lip, and this is complete.
- Girls start to sweat more.
- Girls often get acne – a skin condition that shows up as different types of spots, including whiteheads, blackheads, and pus-filled spots called pustules.
- They have white vaginal discharge
- Girls go through a growth spurt – from the time their periods start, girls grow 5 to 7.5cm (2 to 3 inches) annually over next year or two, then reach their adult height
- Most girls gain weight (which is normal) as their body shape changes – girls develop more body fat along their upper arms, thighs, and upper back; their hips grow rounder and their waist gets narrower

After about 4 years of puberty in girls

- Breasts become adult-like.
- Pubic hair has spread to the inner thigh
- Genitals should now be fully developed
- Girls stop growing taller
- Puberty is completed usually within 3 to 4 years of its onset, and the final height resulting from the complete fusion of the epiphyses occurs within approximately 2 years after menarche.

"Each moment of joy is small, but over time, they add up to more than the sum of their parts."

CHAPTER THREE

Disorders Of Puberty

What is the normal process of Puberty?

- Puberty is the process a child's body goes through as it develops into an adult's body.
- Puberty starts when the body begins producing extra amounts of hormones, leading to physical and emotional changes.
- In girls, these changes include breast development, pubic hair growth, the beginning of menstrual periods, and a growth spurt.
- While every girl will grow and develop at a different rate, the normal onset of puberty is between the ages of 8 and 13.

What is a puberty disorder?

A puberty disorder is when these processes and changes don't occur as they normally should. Disorders of puberty can profoundly impact physical and psychosocial well-being.

Types of Puberty Disorders:

1. **Precocious puberty** – puberty begins too early, before age 7 or 8 in girls.
2. **Delayed puberty** – puberty hasn't started by age 13.
3. **Contra-sexual pubertal development** - development of male characteristics in females
4. **Premature Thelarche** – breast development without any other signs of puberty.

5. **Premature menarche** – periods start without any other signs of puberty.
6. **Premature Adrenarche** – the appearance of pubic hair without any other signs of puberty.

Causes & Risk Factors:

- Heredity
- Hormonal disorders – including polycystic ovary syndrome (POS).
- Genetic disorders.
- Problems in the pituitary or thyroid glands that produce the hormones necessary for body growth and development.
- Chromosome disorders that interfere with normal growth processes.
- Eating disorders.
- Excessive exercise.
- Tumors.
- Infections.
- Chemotherapy.
- Other underlying medical conditions or injury

Precocious puberty
What is precocious puberty?

- Puberty that happens early is called precocious puberty.
- This means a child's physical signs of sexual maturity develop too soon.
- This includes breast growth, pubic hair, and voice changes. These are known as secondary sexual characteristics.
- Precocious puberty happens before age 8 in girls, and before age 9 in boys.
- Most children with the disorder grow fast at first. But they also stop growing before reaching their full genetic height potential.

What causes precocious puberty?

- Tumors or growths on the ovaries, adrenal glands, pituitary gland, or brain.
- Central nervous system problems.
- Family history of the disease, or Certain rare genetic syndromes.
- In many cases, - in 90% of cases it is idiopathic, and no cause can be found for the disorder.

Types of precocious puberty:

1. **Gonadotropin-dependent**

    - This is also known as central precocious puberty. This is the most common type of precocious puberty. Most girls and half of the boys with precocious puberty have this type.
    - Puberty is started by the early secretion of hormones called gonadotropins.
    - Gonadotropins include luteinizing hormone (LH) and follicle stimulation hormone (FSH).
    - In girls, precocious puberty may be caused by the early maturity of the hypothalamus,
    - Pituitary glands, and ovaries. But in most cases, no cause can be found.

2. **Gonadotropin-independent**

    - This is a form of precocious puberty that is not started by the early release of gonadotropins. Instead, it's caused by the early secretion of **high levels of sex hormones.** These include male androgens and female oestrogens.

Who is at risk for precocious puberty?

A child is at risk for precocious puberty if he or she has any of these:

- Tumors or growths on the ovaries, testes, adrenal glands, pituitary gland, or brain.
- Central nervous system problems.
- Family history of the disease.
- A rare genetic syndrome.
- Precocious puberty is more common in females.
- The hormone that is responsible for changes in puberty.

    - In females estrogen and excessive production of oestrogen is the cause of precocious puberty.

What are the signs of precocious puberty?
The signs are secondary sexual characteristics that happen early.
Common in girls:

- Breast growth
- Pubic and underarm hair growth
- Menstruation
- Ovulation

Common signs in boys:

- Enlarging penis and testicles
- Pubic and underarm hair growth
- Facial hair
- Spontaneous erections
- Production of sperm
- Acne
- Deepening of the voice

Other signs of the disorder:
How is precocious puberty diagnosed?

- Moodiness
- Increased aggression

- Growing taller earlier than other classmates
- Child's symptoms and health history.
- Family's health history.
- Child's physical exam.
- Blood tests to measure levels of hormones such as:
    - Luteinizing hrmone (LH)
    - Follicle stimulating hormone (FSH)
    - Oestradiol
    - Testosterone
    - Thyroid hormones
    - **GnRH**: Gonadotropin-stimulating hormone (GnRH) is produced by the hypothalamus in the brain.
- It causes the pituitary gland to release gonadotropins. These then cause sex hormones to be made by the ovaries in girls, or the testes in boys. The GnRH blood test may show the type of precocious puberty.

Bone age radiography (X-ray): This test uses a small amount of radiation to make images of tissues inside the body. An X-ray may be done of the left hand and wrist. This can estimate a child's bone age. With precocious puberty, bone age is often older than calendar age.

Ultrasound. This test uses sound waves and a computer to create images of blood vessels, tissues, and organs. This may be done to look at the adrenal glands and ovaries or testes.

MRI. This test uses large magnets and a computer to make detailed images of tissues in the body. Brain magnetic resonance imaging should be performed in girls younger than six years, all boys with precocious puberty, and children with neurologic symptoms.

What are the possible complications of precocious puberty?

Early puberty will cause a child's body and moods to change much sooner than his or her friends and classmates. This may make a child feel self-conscious and embarrassed, or be teased by other children.

How to manage precocious puberty?

- Treating the child like normal
- Boosting a child's self-esteem and
- Seeking a child counselor if more help is needed

How is precocious puberty treated?

The goal of treatment is to stop the onset of early puberty signs. In some cases, the signs can be reversed.

Treatment will depend on the type of precocious puberty and the cause.

Treatment may be done with synthetic gonadotropin-releasing hormone. This can stop the sexual maturity process. It can be done by stopping the pituitary gland from releasing the gonadotropin hormones.

When to consult the child's healthcare provider?

Consult the child's healthcare provider if signs of sexual development are seen in a girl before age 8 or in a boy before age 9.

Delayed puberty

Puberty starts when the pituitary gland begins to produce two hormones, luteinizing hormone (called LH) and follicle-stimulating hormone (called FSH), which cause the ovaries to enlarge and begin producing estrogens.

The growth spurt starts shortly after breasts begin to develop, and the first menstrual cycle begins about 2-3 years later.

Delayed puberty in girls

A girl who has not started to have breast development by the age of 13 is considered to be having delayed puberty.

What are the causes of delayed puberty in girls?

Constitutional delayed puberty:

Some girls with delayed puberty simply mature late, but once they start, puberty will progress normally. This is called constitutional delayed puberty and is more common in boys than girls.

Hereditary:

Sometimes puberty is inherited from the parents, so it is more likely to occur if the mother started her periods after age 14 (the average is about 12 ½) or if the father matured late.

Body fat:

Decreased body fat is a major cause of pubertal delay in girls. It can be seen in very athletic girls, particularly gymnasts, ballet dancers, and competitive swimmers.

Anorexia nervosa: It can also be seen in girls with anorexia nervosa, who engage in extreme dieting or binging and purging because they fear becoming too fat even when they are abnormally thin.

Finally, it can be seen in several chronic illnesses in which body fat is often decreased.

Ovarian disorders:

Primary ovarian insufficiency:

Some girls with delayed puberty may have problems with their ovaries. The ovaries are either not developing properly or are being damaged. This is referred to as primary ovarian insufficiency.

- Turner syndrome:
    - The major cause present at birth is Turner syndrome, in which all or part of one of the two X chromosomes is missing.
    - Most girls with Turner syndrome are also extremely short for their age and may have certain distinctive physical features, such as webbing of the neck, a high-arched palate, or arms that bend outward when extended.
    - In the majority of cases, Turner syndrome is diagnosed before the age of 13 because of short stature.

Secondary ovarian insufficiency:

Ovarian insufficiency can be acquired. The major acquired cause of ovarian insufficiency is **damage to the ovaries** as a result of

radiation, usually to treat leukemia or certain other kinds of cancer.

Lack of pituitary hormones:

Sometimes, girls may have their ovaries damaged by the body's immune system. Some girls fail to start puberty because of a lack of the pituitary hormones LH and FSH, also called gonadotropins.

Ovarian insufficiency can occur when there are other pituitary deficiencies also, including growth hormone. It can be an isolated finding (particularly in a girl whose puberty is delayed but not short).

How is delayed puberty in girls diagnosed? Blood tests:

- Measure levels of LH, FSH, estradiol, and, in some cases, other tests.
- Very high levels of LH and FSH will indicate that the ovaries are not working properly, and the pituitary is trying to stimulate them to work harder.
- If the LH, FSH, and estradiol are all low, the problem could be either decreased body fat (if one of the risk factors listed above is present) or a permanent deficiency of LH and FSH.

Karyotype:

If the cause of ovarian insufficiency is not clear, a chromosome study or karyotype will be done to see if all or some cells are missing all or part of an X chromosome.

Other tests may be ordered if a deficiency of multiple pituitary hormones is suspected,

MRI: Sometimes, a brain MRI may be helpful.

X-Ray: A hand X-ray for bone age is often done, which is typically delayed by 2 or more years, which means that there is still additional time to grow.

How is delayed puberty in girls treated?

In girls with constitutional delayed puberty, breast development will start on its own later. Giving oestrogen for 4-6 months is sometimes used to help get things started sooner.

For girls with delayed puberty and decreased body fat: Sometimes eating more and **gaining weight** will help get puberty started.

For girls with primary ovarian insufficiency or a permanent deficiency of gonadotropins: Long-term oestrogen replacement is needed and can be given either in the form of a daily tablet of oestradiol or as a patch that needs to be applied to the skin twice a week.

Usually, a low dose is started and often the dose is increased about every 6 months.

After 12-18 months, a second hormone called progestin (for example, Provera) is usually started.

After a few months, it may result in a period, usually within a day or two of stopping the progestin.

Delayed puberty in boys

If the secondary sexual characteristics do not appear by age 14 years in males, it is called delayed puberty.

Delayed puberty is more common in males. Signs and symptoms of delayed puberty

Delayed puberty is defined by signs (lack of increase in testicle size by age 14).

Children often consult for an evaluation because they're concerned that they're not growing as quickly as their peers.

What are the causes of delayed puberty in boys?

1. Constitutional growth delay (CGD) :CGD is a temporary delay in skeletal growth, which keeps a child from being as tall as his peers, at least for a while.

- Among boys, around 60 percent of the time, delayed puberty is caused by constitutional growth delay.
- It's hard to say for sure, but CGD is thought to affect around twice as many boys as girls.
- CGD is a normal variant of growth, but may still make a child feel distressed.

- As we grow up, our bones **"mature."** If a child has CGD, a doctor can look at an **x-ray of his hand** and **wrist**, and see that his bones appear "younger" than expected for his chronological age.
- CGD is often inherited. If one or both parents were **"late-bloomers**," it's likely that their child may also mature late.
- Kids with CGD go through puberty and reach an appropriate adult height, just not as quickly as their peers do.

2.An underlying medical condition

- Cardiac conditions.
- Chronic illness: cystic fibrosis, sickle cell anemia, celiac disease, etc.
- Certain genetic conditions, such as Klinefelter's syndrome in boys and Turner syndrome in girls.

3.Some psychiatric medications can also contribute to delayed puberty.

- Anxicty.
- Depression.

4.Prevention of "Start Puberty Signal

Conditions that prevent the hypothalamus or pituitary gland from sending the **"Start puberty"** Signal and conditions that prevent the ovaries or testes from being able to respond to the "start puberty" Signal

5. Acquired: Radiation therapy,

Testicular surgery, Ovarian surgery

Treatment: Treatment is giving pulsatile GnRH

Contra-sexual pubertal development:

- It is a condition where a male or female child develops characteristics of the opposite gender.
- **Girls (Virilization)** can develop a deep voice or facial hair.

- **Boys (feminization)** mainly develop breasts (gynecomastia).
- Contra-sexual development can also interrupt puberty milestones, including growth.

Symptoms: Differ between males and females.
Females (virilization)

- Facial hair
- Excess of pubic hair
- Unusually large muscles
- Deep voice
- Irregular menstruation (periods)
- Rapid growth

Causes:
There may be hormonal changes in females :

- 21-hydroxylase deficiency – this inherited disorder affects the adrenal glands that produce hormones; females with this condition produce too many androgens (male sex hormones).
- Acromegaly – a disorder that is the result of too much growth hormone.
- Congenital adrenal hyperplasia – is an inherited disorder that affects the adrenal glands due to a lack of necessary enzymes.
- Cushing's syndrome (disease) – a rare condition that occurs when there is too much cortisol (stress hormone).
- Excess testosterone – the adrenal glands will produce too many androgens (testosterone) if there is a tumor in the gland or if the adrenal gland is enlarged.
- Hyperthyroidism – the gland that regulates metabolism (thyroid) can alter hormones.
- Hyperprolactinemia – a disorder that is the result of too much prolactin (amino acid responsible for milk production).
- Medications – steroids, antibiotics, chemotherapy, or heart medications.

- Ovarian or adrenal gland tumors – benign (non-cancerous) or malignant (cancerous) tumors can block or change hormone production.
- Polycystic ovary syndrome (POS)– this hormonal condition causes enlarged ovaries and cysts.

Males (Feminization)

The main symptom of contrasexual pubertal development in males is the development of breast tissue **(gynecomastia).**

Causes:

- There are several reasons there may be hormonal changes in males, including:
- Liver or kidney failure – hormonal changes in response to medicines and dialysis.
- Malnutrition or starvation – poor nutrition causes testosterone to drop, but estrogen remains constant.
- Medications – steroids, antibiotics, chemotherapy, or heart medications.
- Street drugs and alcohol – such as marijuana, heroin, and amphetamine.
- Tumors – on the testes, adrenal glands, or pituitary glands.

Premature Thelarche

Premature thelarche is a benign condition that affects young girls and may be interpreted as a sign of central precocious puberty (CPP).

Parental concern is common when breast development is noted in a young girl.

It is important to differentiate premature thelarche from CPP, as the latter is a more serious disorder that may affect final adult height and menarcheal age, and may have psychological implications as well. Distinguishing between the two conditions clinically may help the patients avoid unnecessary testing.

Pediatricians can play a pivotal role by providing reassurance to families and helping alleviate parental anxiety.

What causes premature thelarche?

The exact cause of the condition is still unknown, but it has been linked to a variety of **genetic, dietary** and **physiological** factors.

The condition may be from **sensitivity to oestrogen**, or it can be a symptom of **hormonal imbalances in the adrenal glands or ovaries.**

Premature Menarche

Pre-pubertal vaginal bleeding is considered isolated menarche when, in the absence of detectable abnormality, it is not accompanied by any evidence of sexual development. The etiology remains unclear.

Adrenarche

Adrenarche means **"the awakening of the adrenal gland."** The adrenal gland is responsible for making hormones including androgens—sex hormones that cause changes such as the **development of pubic hair, oily skin, oily hair,** and **body odor**.

There is one adrenal gland on top of each kidney.

What causes premature Adrenarche?

Premature adrenarche is caused when the adrenal gland begins secreting sex hormones called androgens earlier than normal.

In most cases, it's not that more androgen is being made, it's that the standard amount is being made earlier than normal.

- That means that in most cases, the effects of adrenarche are not exaggerated (your child won't be hairier than her peers), the effects simply appear sooner.
- It's not known what causes the adrenal gland to begin secreting androgens early.
- Since exposure to these hormones causes premature Adrenarche, the child may also experience it if she comes in contact with hormone creams or other hormonal medications.

Testing & Diagnosis

How is premature Adrenarche diagnosed?

- If a child is showing symptoms of premature Adrenarche, she can be simply monitored for some time with regular check-ups.
- Other diagnostic procedures may be performed to rule out causes and complications. These could include:
- Monitoring the child's growth patterns to see if she is growing at a steady rate
- Blood tests to measure hormone levels
- X-ray of the child's hand to determine "bone age," which can indicate early puberty

Premature Adrenarche -Treatments

- Premature adrenarche doesn't require treatment. However, it will cause the child's body to change sooner than those of her peers, and this may make her feel self-conscious.
- It's important to reassure her that the changes in her body are completely normal, even if she is experiencing them earlier than other children.
- Helping the child cope with teasing from her peers, treating her appropriately for her age, and boosting her self-esteem are all important ways of helping her adjust well.

Some concerns

1. **What action to be taken if a child's puberty is delayed?**

    - Children with delayed puberty should be evaluated by a specialist, but most often, it is not a matter of concern. Even if the child has an underlying medical condition, puberty can almost always be started through hormone therapy.
    - Most often, it only requires brief treatment to start puberty, but in some cases, longterm hormone therapy will be recommended.

2. **If a child has no breast development even after pubic hair and body odour are developed, is there anything to be worried about?**

    - If a child has pubic hair and body odour and no breast development, she should be evaluated.
    - This is because while they tend to happen around the same time, the development of breasts and the development of public hair/body odour are two separate processes, each triggered by their hormones.
    - The diagnosis of delayed puberty only takes into account the process and the hormones that lead to breast development.

3. **Will delayed puberty affect a child's ultimate growth and development?**

    It can affect:

Children with CGD tend to not grow as much during their growth spurts as other children, which may make them a little smaller than adults.

4. **Is delayed puberty harmful?**

- Delayed puberty is not harmful. Since there are medical causes, Children with delayed puberty should be evaluated, but most of the time it's not a medical problem.
- Still, if the child feels as though he's not keeping up with his peers in growth and physical development, it can be very upsetting. These feelings should be taken seriously.

5. **Will delayed puberty affect the child's reproductive function?**

- It depends on what's causing the delay. If the delay is temporary, like in CGD, it typically doesn't affect fertility. Certain medical conditions that affect hormones can cause problems with fertility, and researchers are working on how to improve fertility in these cases.

"Speak 5 lines to yourself every morning
God is always with me, Today is my day, I am the winner, I can do it"
-APJ Abdul Kalam, Former Hon. President of India

CHAPTER FOUR

Puberty & Adolescence - Hormonal Changes

Maturation of the neural mechanisms in the brain which regulate the **pulsatile secretion of gonadotropin-releasing hormone** by the hypothalamus causes a transformation from an immature to a mature state.

The neural mechanism is termed the **GnRH pulse generator**. The signal or signals responsible for the maturation of the GnRH pulse generator have not been identified.

Hormones and the Body

- How does the body know to grow?
- What happens n the inside that makes us change n the outside?

Any complex process usually requires an organized system to manage all the moving parts.

When you listen to a symphony, for example, many different instruments must play the right notes at the right times to produce the beautiful music we hear.

For all these separate elements to work together, a conductor tells each instrument what, when, and how to play.

In the body, **our genes are like musical notes** that are strung together to make each body's own unique song.

When the appropriate time comes, **special chemicals called hormones** (Made in one part of the body, an endocrine gland, and then travel through the blood to tell other parts of the body what to do.) are like **conductors** that tell other parts of the body what to do.

The many **organ systems** in the body are then like the **instruments** that carry out the conductor's commands and bring the entire process to life.

During these intricate periods of transition, **hormones serve as messengers** that travel throughout the body and give orders to grow (or stop growing), change shape and size, or make more (or less) of something the body needs.

What Happens during Puberty?

Puberty is a period of a series of hormone-driven changes that happen in our bodies, right before and during adolescence, the time when we grow from children into adults.

The shape, size, and composition of our bodies change as we progress toward sexual maturity, which is the ability of an organism to reproduce. Our moods and behaviors change as a result of puberty as well.

The same hormones that cause changes in our bodies also help shape the structure and organization of our brains.

Through puberty, our brains strengthen and fine-tune the connections that allow for mature ways of thinking, feeling, and behaving.

What are the different hormones involved in pubertal changes?

Gonadotropin-Releasing Hormone (GnRH), FSH, LH

- GnRH produced in Hypothalamus regulates the Follicle stimulating hormone (FSH)and Luteinizing hormone(LH), produced by the Pituitary gland
- The increase in FSH is much less marked than that of LH. The primary triggering that initiates the activation of the

hypothalamic-pituitary-gonadal axis at puberty is still hypothetical.

- One of the important neuroendocrine mechanisms that control the onset of puberty is probably an increase in the frequency of GnRH pulse stimulation of the pituitary.
- Whatever the mechanism, the process is not abrupt but develops over several years, as evidenced by slowly rising plasma concentrations of the gonadotropins and testosterone or estrogens.
- The first demonstrable biological change of puberty is the appearance of pulsatile LH release during sleep.
- As puberty progresses, the frequency and amplitude of LH secretory peaks increase, although peaks are also found during the wake period.
- At the end of puberty, the difference between sleep and wake LH secretory patterns disappears.
- In girls, circulating FSH levels increase progressively from 10 to 11 years of age (stage P2), approximately 1 year prior to those of LH.
- Thereafter, gonadotropins continue to increase throughout puberty, but important fluctuations are observed in relation to the menstrual cycle.
- In boys, a significant increase in both plasma FSH and LH is also found from the onset of puberty (stage P2), closely linked to the rapid increase in testicular size.

Characteristic of this pubertal stage:

A further significant increase in circulating gonadotropins is also observed at late puberty (stages P4 and P5).

Actions of FSH in brief –For M/F

- Stimulates gametogenesis
- Stimulates the development of the primary ovarian follicle
- Increases estrogen production

Actions of L.H in brief-For M/F

- Stimulates testicular Leydig cells to produce testosterone.
- Stimulates ovarian theca cells to produce androgens and the corpus luteum to synthesize Progesterone.
- Mid-cycle surge leads to ovulation.

Actions of Prolactin in brief

- Serum prolactin concentrations increase modestly during female puberty but remain stable in boys.
- The physiological role of prolactin in the course of puberty, if any, is unknown.

Actions of Adrenal Steroids in brief

- Adrenal androgens vary from infancy through adolescence. This phenomenon is called Adrenarche.
- In girls, dehydroepiandrosterone (DHEA) and dehydroepiandrosterone sulfate (DHEAS) increase as early as 6 to 7 years of age, followed within 1 to 2 years by a concomitant increase in androstenedione.
- In boys, DHEA and DHEAS increase as early as 8 to 9 years of age, followed by androstenedione 1 to 2 years later. Adrenarche begins before the rise in gonadotropin secretion.
- The adrenal androgens are responsible for the appearance of axillary hair and, in part, for the appearance of pubic hair in the adolescent; however, they do not appear to play a decisive role in determining the initiation of puberty.

Actions of Estradiol

- The rising levels of plasma gonadotropins stimulate the ovary to produce increasing amounts of estradiol.

- Estradiol is responsible for the development of secondary sexual characteristics, that is, growth and development of the breasts and reproductive organs, fat redistribution (hips, breasts), and bone maturation.
- The maturation of the ovary at adolescence correlates well with estradiol secretion and the stages of puberty.
- In prepuberty, the ovarian size volume extends from 0.5 cm. (0.3 to 0.9 cm3) to 1.0 cm3 or more, indicating that puberty has begun.

- During puberty, the ovarian size increases rapidly to a mean postpubertal volume of 4.0 cm3 (1.8 to 5.3 cm3).
- The **pre-pubertal uterus is tear-drop shaped**, with the neck and isthmus accounting for up to two-thirds of the uterine volume; then, with the production of oestrogens, it becomes **pear-shaped**, with the uterine body increasing in length and thickness proportionately more than the cervix.

- During puberty, plasma **oestradiol levels fluctuate widely,** probably reflecting successive waves of follicular development that fail to reach the ovulatory stage.
- The uterine endometrium is affected by these changes and undergoes **cycles of proliferation and regression** until a point is reached when substantial growth occurs so that **withdrawal of oestrogen results in the first menstruation (Menarche)**.
- Plasma testosterone levels also increase at puberty although not as markedly as in males.
- Plasma progesterone remains at low levels even if secondary sexual characteristics have appeared. A rise in progesterone after menarche is, in general, indicative that ovulation has occurred.
- The first ovulation does not take place until 6-9 months after menarche because the positive feedback mechanism of estrogen is not developed.

Actions of oestradiol in brief:

- Stimulates the development of the uterus, vagina, and labia.
- Stimulates the development of breast ducts.
- A high level increases rates of epiphyseal fusion while a low level increases linear growth.
- Increases fat tissue in the body
- Triggers mid-cycle surge of LH
- Stimulates the development of proliferative endometrium of the uterus

Actions of Progesterone in brief:

- Stimulates lobular and alveolar breast development. Converts proliferative endometrium to secretory endometrium.

Testosterone

The increase in testicular size observed during prepuberty and puberty results essentially from the development of the seminiferous tubules under the stimulating effect of FSH.

- The testicular volume increases throughout puberty up to Tanner stage P4 when a longitudinal diameter of 5.0 + 0.5 cm or a volume of 17.6 + 4.0 ml is reached.Long-standing pulsatile LH secretion induces the differentiation of interstitial cells into testosterone-secreting Leydig cells, which, in turn, exert a negative feedback control on LH secretion. As puberty progresses, spermatogenesis is initiated and then sustained by FSH and by testosterone produced by the Leydig cells under LH control.
- A significant increase of plasma testosterone is found only between Tanner pubertal stages P3 and P4.

Actions of Testosterone in brief Both male and female

- Increases linear growth.
- Stimulates the growth of pubic and axillary hair

Male:

- Accelerates the fusion of the epiphysis.
- Stimulates the development of the penis, scrotum, prostate, and seminal vesicles.
- Stimulates growth of facial hair.
- Increases the size of the larynx and deepens the voice.
- Increases secretion of sebaceous glands.
- Increases libido.
- Increases muscle mass and red cell mass.

Role of GH, IGF-I, and Insulin in Puberty

- There is ample evidence that GH plays a role in pubertal development.
- GH stimulates FSH-induced differentiation of granulosa cells directly, increases ovarian levels of IGF-I, and amplifies the ovarian response to gonadotropins.
- IGF-I, in turn, enhances the gonadotropin effect on the granulosa cell, and GH seems to act synergistically with a still-developing pattern of gonadotropin secretion to facilitate ovarian maturation post-menarche.
- Local production or accumulation of GH and IGF-I exerts intraovarian paracrine control on steroidogenesis.
- Puberty of patients with isolated GH deficiency is frequently delayed, Leydig cell function is diminished, and the response to chorionic gonadotropins is decreased.
- GH administration can restore testicular responsiveness to LH and Leydig cell steroidogenesis.
- Growth hormone-releasing factor (GRF) levels and GH secretion increase considerably during puberty, mainly at night.

- The amplitude of GH peaks increases early in puberty. IGF-I is an important modulator of growth during childhood and adolescence.
- Adrenal androgens seem to have no physiological role in normal growth.
- The characteristic pubertal growth spurt results mainly from the synergetic effect of gonadal sex steroids, growth hormone, and IGF-I production, with all showing a significant increase at the time of pubertal growth acceleration.
- Insulin is also important for normal growth. Plasma insulin levels increase throughout childhood, but the rise is particularly pronounced during puberty with a strong positive correlation with IGF-I.

"Life has got all those twists and turns. You've got to hold on tight and off you go."

—Nicole Kidman

CHAPTER FIVE

Nutrition in Adolescents

Eating healthy food is important at any age, but it's especially important for adolescents.

The growth and development of adolescents depend to a large extent on their nutrition.

As adolescents' body is still growing, it is important that they eat enough good quality food and the right kinds to meet their energy and nutrition needs.

As adolescents start to become more independent, they make their own food choices.

The complex myriad of physiological as well as psychological changes, accompanied by rapid growth and an increase in physical activity, create special nutritional needs that are higher during adolescence than at any other time in life.

Failure to consume adequately at this time in life can potentially retard physical growth, and intellectual capacity and delay sexual maturation.

Adolescence also offers a second opportunity for children to achieve their full genetic potential for growth.

In developing countries, nutrition in adolescence is of particular significance since the population of young people and adolescents is large.

The nutrition of female adolescents is of special importance, given the far-reaching effects of maternal undernutrition.

The pregestational nutritional status as well as nutrition during pregnancy is an important factor determining the health of the next generation.

The saying "**We are what we eat**" has changed to "**We are what our mother ate.**"

What is the global status of nutrition in adolescents?

Studies reported that malnutrition is common in adolescents, those in developing countries suffer from undernutrition, while those in developed countries face social pressure for achieving a body image that fits the popular beauty model.

On the other extreme, other adolescents who are obese, grow up to develop chronic diseases and burden the health care system.

What is Nutrition?

Nutrition is the study of how our body uses the food we eat.

Good nutrition requires a satisfactory diet, which is capable of supporting the individual consuming it, in a state of good health by providing the desired nutrients in required amounts.

The average nutritional requirements of groups of people are fixed and depend on age, sex, height, weight, degree of activity, and rate of growth. Food provides the energy and nutrients we need to be healthy.

Nutritional Requirements

- Nutrition in Adolescence should meet the following objectives:
- Provide the necessary nutrients to meet the demands of physical and intellectual growth
- Provide adequate stores for illness, or pregnancy
- Prevent adult-onset diseases related to nutrition eg. hypertension and osteoporosis.
- Encourage healthy eating habits and lifestyle Adolescent nutrition

Why good nutrition is important for adolescents?

All individuals have two growth phases during their lifetime at **infancy** and **adolescence**. Hence adolescents have Developmental changes that occur in full swing and they have increased requirements for nutrients like vitamins and minerals.

During this growing phase of life, they gain 50% of their adult weight and 25% of their height.

They need strength and energy as they always are running, jumping, working, and playing with vigor and enthusiasm.

Changes in lifestyle and eating behaviors.

Psychological changes occurring due to peer pressure and the generation gap between parents and children impact on adolescents' nutrition.

Why do Adolescent girls need a more nutritious diet than adolescent boys?

Adolescent Girls lose blood every month during menstruation.

In societies where early marriage and childbirth are norms,

Adolescent Girls require a more nutritious diet during pregnancy and while breastfeeding.

Types of Nutrients:

Macro Nutrients

- Carbohydrates
- Proteins
- Fats

Micronutrients:

- Vitamins
- Minerals
- Water

Food:

- Food is anything solid or liquid that has a chemical composition that enables it, when swallowed, to do one or more of the following:
- Provide the body with the material from which it can produce heat or any form of energy.

- Provide material to allow growth, maintenance, repair, or reproduction to proceed.
- Supply substances that protect the body from disease and degeneration.

Composition of food:

- Carbohydrates are the most important source of energy contributing to 50-60% of the total energy requirement.
- Protein requirement is determined by lean body mass which provides 10-15% of the total energy requirement.
- Fats should provide no more than the total energy requirement of which saturated fat should be <10%
- Vitamins, minerals, and other micronutrients are essential for normal body functioning.Iron is required to prevent anemia and heme sources are better than non-heme iron.
- Enzymes need Zinc. Calcium is needed for bone health and its absorption peaks around puberty.
- Dietary fiber intake should be 15.5-34.5 G/day for adolescent males and 16-28.5 G/day for adolescent females.
- Fluid is required to maintain hydration. Carbohydrates: Carbohydrates are one of the main types of food.

Carbohydrates

- Carbohydrates are categorized into simple and complex, depending on how fast your body digests and absorbs the sugar.

Sources:

- Simple carbohydrates: grains, fruits, milk products, and table sugar.
- Complex carbohydrates: Whole grain bread and cereals, starchy vegetables, and legumes.

Functions:

- Foods containing Complex carbohydrates and some simple carbohydrates provide vitamins, minerals, and fiber also.
- The liver breaks down carbohydrates into glucose (blood sugar) and the body uses this sugar for energy for the cells, tissues, and organs.

Calories requirement:

Age Group 13-15 yrs

Boys: 2860 Kcal

Girls: 2400Kcal

Age Group 16-18 yrs

Boys: 3200Kcl

Girls: 2800Kcl

Adolescents who consume 45 to 65 percent of their calories from carbs will meet their needs. For example, an adolescent girl who eats 2,000 calories per day requires 225 to 325 grams of carbs (carbs provide 4 calories per gram), and an adolescent boy consuming 2,600 calories a day needs about 293 to 423 grams of carbohydrates daily.

Proteins:

Sources:

Meat, fish. cheese, eggs, Beans, Nuts, seeds, and certain grains.

Animal proteins or complete proteins or 1st class proteins: Proteins from meat and other animal products supply all of the amino acids the body can't make on its own.

Plant proteins are incomplete proteins or 2nd class proteins, that lack one or more essential amino acids— fruits, vegetables, grains, and nuts.

Functions:

- Protein is present in every living cell in the body, in muscle, bone, skin, hair, and virtually every other body part or tissue.

- Our bodies need protein from the foods we eat to build and maintain bones, muscles, and skin and to produce enzymes, hormones, antibodies, and the globin part of hemoglobin.
- You must combine them to get all of the amino acids your body needs.

Note: It is important to get enough dietary protein. You need to eat protein every day because your body doesn't store it the way it stores fats or carbohydrates.

RDA Protein:

The average person needs **50 to 65 grams** of protein each day

Age Group 13-15 yrs
Girls: 43 gms
Boys: 45 gms

Age Group 16-18yrs
Boys: 55 gms
Girls: 46 gms

Fats or Lipids:

Categories of fats:

1. Monounsaturated fat
2. Polyunsaturated fat
3. Saturated fat

Sources:

Saturated fat:

Red meat-beef, lamb, pork, Skin- chicken and other poultry, Whole milk dairy products like cheese and butter. Eggs, Palm, and coconut oils

Unsaturated fats:

Avocado, Canola oil, Salmon fish, Olive oil, Peanuts, Nuts such as almonds, hazelnuts, and pecans.

Seeds such as pumpkins and sesame seeds

Functions of fat:

- Fat is a major source of energy and aids your body in absorbing vitamins.
- It's important for proper growth, and development and for keeping you healthy.
- Fat provides taste to foods and helps you feel full.
- Fats are an especially important source of calories and nutrients for infants and adolescents.
- Intake of fats depends upon total calories required30- 35% of Total Kcal>10% from saturated fats.

RDA

Age Group 13-15 yrs.

Boys: 45gms

Girls: 40gms

Age Group 16-17 yrs

Boys: 50gms

Girls: 35gms

An increase in fat consumption leads to:

- Obesity
- Cardiovascular disease

You should try to avoid Saturated fats such as butter and Trans fats - some margarine, crackers, cookies, snack foods, and other foods made with or fried in partially hydrogenated oils

Vitamins and Minerals:

Vitamins are substances that our body needs to grow and develop normally.

Vitamins are natural substances found in plants and animals.

Our body uses these substances to stay healthy and support its many functions.

There are 13 vitamins your body needs. They are vitamins A, C, D, E, and K, and the B vitamins (thiamine, riboflavin, niacin, pantothenic acid, biotin, vitamin B-6, vitamin B-12, and folate).

What are the categories of Vitamins?

Fat-soluble

Water-soluble.

Fat-soluble vitamins— A, D, E, and K — dissolve in fat and can be stored in the body fat. When the body needs them, it takes them out of storage to be used.

Water-soluble vitamins— C and the B-complex

- Vitamins (such as vitamins B6, B12, niacin, riboflavin, and folate)—need to dissolve in water before the body can absorb them. Because of this, your body can't store these vitamins.
- Any vitamin that the body doesn't use as it passes through your system, is lost in motion mostly. So you need a fresh supply of these vitamins every day.
- You can usually get all your vitamins from the foods you eat.
- Your body can also make vitamins D and K. People who eat a vegetarian diet may need to take a vitamin B12 supplement.
- Each vitamin has a specific job. If you have low levels of certain vitamins, you may develop a deficiency disease.

Vitamin. A Sources:

Carrots, Papaya, Meat, Cheese, Eggs, Sweet potato, Squash, Broccoli, Fish, Mangoes, Peppers, apricots, Peaches, Melon, Avocados.

Functions:

Vit. A. is important for normal vision, the immune system, and reproduction.

Vit. A also helps the heart, lungs, kidneys, and other organs work properly.

RDA for both boys and Girls:

- Retinol-600 mcg
- Beta carotene-4800 mcg

Vitamin. D

Sources: Salmon, Eggs, Fortified cereal, Tuna **Functions:** Improves calcium absorption and bone growth.

RDA: 600 IU for both boys and girls

Vitamin E

Sources: Pomegranate seeds, Sunflower seeds, Avocado Mango Olives and Olive oil, Kiwi, and nuts.

Functions: Antioxidant properties.

RDA: 7.5-10mg

Vitamin K

Sources: Cabbage, Cauliflower, Tomato, Alfa Alfa, Spinach, Green leafy vegetables, Egg yolk, Meat, Liver Cheese, and Dairy products.

Functions:

Blood clotting process:

Vitamin B complex is composed of eight B vitamins:

1. B1 (thiamine)
2. B2 (riboflavin)
3. B3 (niacin)
4. B5 (pantothenic acid)
5. B6 (pyridoxine)
6. B7 (biotin)
7. B9 (folic acid)
8. B12 (cobalamin)

Each of these essential vitamins contributes to your overall bodily function.

Sources: Whole grains, Meat, Milk, Egg, Legumes, Sunflower seeds, Nuts, Leafy vegetables, Avocado, Fish

Functions:

B vitamins play a vital role in maintaining good health and well-being.

As the building blocks of a healthy body, B vitamins have a direct impact on your energy levels, brain function, and cell metabolism.

Vitamin B complex may help prevent infections and help support or promote:

- Cell health
- Growth of red blood cells
- Energy levels
- Eyesight
- Brain function
- Digestion
- Appetite
- Proper nerve function
- Hormones and cholesterol production
- Cardiovascular health

Muscle tone RDA:

- Girls:
    - B1: 1.1 milligrams (mg)
    - B2: 1.1 mg
    - B3: 14 mg NE
    - B5: 5 mg
    - B6: 1.3 mg
    - B12: 2.4 mcg
    - Biotin: 30 micrograms (mcg)
    - Folic acid: 400 mcg DFE
- Boys:
    - B1: 1.2 mg
    - B2: 1.3 mg

- B3: 16 mg NE
- B5: 5 mg
- B6: 1.3 mg
- Biotin: 30 mcg
- Folic acid: 400 mcg DFE
- B12: 2.4 mcg

Vitamin. C. also known as ascorbic acid:

Sources: Citrus fruits, Strawberries, Bell Peppers, Papayas, Leafy vegetables, Kiwi fruit, Broccoli, Guava, Amla, and Tomatoes.

Functions:

- Helps to protect cells and keep them healthy.
- Maintain healthy skin, blood vessels, bones, and cartilage.
- Help wound healing.
- Antioxidant
- Iron absorption

RDA

Age Group 13-15 yrs
Girls: 65 mg
Boys: 70mg.

Age Group 16-18 yrs
Boys: 85mg
Girls: 70 mg

Minerals:

Vitamins are organic substances (made by plants or animals), and **minerals are inorganic elements** that come from the soil and water and are absorbed by plants or eaten by animals.

Your body needs larger amounts of some minerals, such as **calcium and iron**, to grow and stay healthy, and **trace minerals, chromium, copper, iodine, selenium, and zinc.** You only need very small amounts of them each day.

Calcium

Sources: Cheese, Yogurt, Collard Greens, Sardines, Milk, Spinach

Functions:

- Building strong bones and teeth- supports bone and teeth structure
- Clotting blood.
- Sending and receiving nerve signals.
- Squeezing and relaxing muscles.
- Releasing hormones and other chemicals.
- Keeping a normal heartbeat.

RDA:

For both girls and boys: **600-800 mg Iron:**

Sources: Chicken, Liver, Broccoli, Dried beans/Green peas, Pork, Beef, Potatoes with skin, Spinach, Egg yolk, Clams, Iron-fortified cereals, Raisins, Shrimp, Dried apricot, Watermelon

Functions:

- Transporting oxygen in the bloodstream
- Haemoglobin Synthesis
- In girls to support iron loss with the onset of menstruation
- Iron needs are highest in an adolescent growth spurt in males for muscle development and in females after menarche.
- Inadequate intake may lead to iron deficiency anaemia, especially in females

RDA:

Age Group 13-15 yrs
Boys: 22mg
Girls: 30 mg
Age Group 16-17 yrs
Boys: 26mg

Girls: 32mg

Zinc:

Sources: Pumpkin seeds, Chickweed, Mushrooms, yogurt, Spinach, Garlic, grains, Nuts, Meat, Cheese, and Milk.

Functions:

- Vital for growth and sexual maturation
- Deficiency lowers immunity making adolescents more prone to infection

RDA:

Age Group 13-15 yrs
Boys: 14.3 mg
Girls: 12.8 mg
Age Group 16-17 yrs
Boys: 17.6 mg
Girls: 14.2

What do Vitamins and Minerals Do?

- Vitamins and minerals boost the immune system.
- Support normal growth and development and help cells and organs do their jobs.
- They don't yield energy but enable the body to use other nutrients and also play an important role in the growth, repair, and regulation of vital body functions.
- Iron and calcium requirements are particularly increased during adolescence.
- Zinc is needed for growth and sexual maturation.

Water:

Water is needed:

- For the body to be healthy and energetic
- For proper digestion of the food
- For avoiding urinary tract infections
- For avoiding constipation

What is a balanced diet?

A balanced diet is one that provides all nutrients (Carbohydrates, Fats, Proteins, Vitamins, and Minerals) in required amounts and propositions for maintaining health and general well-being and also makes small provisions of nutrients to withstand a short duration of illness.

It can be achieved through a blend of four basic food groups, i.e. carbohydrates, proteins, fats, vitamins, and minerals.

As these are present in different types of food items like pulses, chapatti or rice, green vegetables, and milk, it is important to eat these food items in the right mix every day.

What are the consequences of unhealthy food habits?

Undernutrition and Micro malnutrition cause Protein Energy Malnutrition

- Malnutrition leading to obesity
- Changes in dietary pattern
- Risk of taking restricted calories
- Increased intake of junk food
- Consuming unbalanced and high-fat diets
- Skipping meals
- Fewer intake of protective foods like fruits and veggies.

Nutritional concerns in adolescents

- Iron deficiency anaemia (global anaemic prevalence in school-going children is 25.4%).
- Vit. A, Calcium and iodine deficiency is generally found in adolescents

- Obesity is one of the major public health issues which poses an increased risk of diabetes, hyperlipidemia, Over nutrition, and Cardiovascular disorders. (18% of children and adolescents)
- Polycystic ovarian syndrome(PCOS)

Consequences of malnutrition:

Retardation of physical growth and intellectual development.

Delay in sexual maturation.

Obesity, obesity-related chronic diseases, osteoporosis, and eating disorders.

ANEMIA:

Anaemia is having less than a normal number of red blood cells and less haemoglobin than normal in the blood.

Normal HB% for men-14.4gms.% and for women- 12.5-14.5gms.%

More than 70% of girls in the age group 10-19 years in developing countries suffer from severe or moderate anaemia.

Causes of anaemia:

1. **Deficient intake or loss of nutrients:** Iron deficiency anaemia is common in infants and young children because of taking diet deficient or lacking iron. Diarrhoeal diseases or hookworm infestation cause loss of nutrients.
2. **Blood loss:** Girls are more likely than boys to have anaemia because of the loss of blood each month through menstruation and frequent pregnancies, abortions and childbirth, Postpartum haemorrhage (Excessive blood loss after delivery), and Breastfeeding.
3. Chronic blood loss from menstruation or from small amounts of repeated bleeding.
4. Anaemia can also be due to gastrointestinal bleeding caused by medications.
5. **Genetic or acquired defects or disease:** Hereditary blood diseases like sickle cell anaemia, thalassemia, etc. genetic in

origin.

6. Acute blood loss from

    a. Internal bleeding(as from a bleeding ulcer) or
    b. External bleeding (as from trauma / Piles) can produce anaemia in an amazingly short span of time.

7. Malaria Serious disease:
8. Certain diseases can hurt the body's ability to make red blood cells. For eg, people with kidney disease, especially those getting dialysis, are at higher risk for developing anaemia. Their kidneys can't create enough hormones to make blood cells and iron is lost in dialysis

Physiological and social aspects of Anemia Eating patterns of Adolescents

- The Independent phase of life, which influences food behavior, also breaks away from family eating patterns.
- Family meals become less important.
- Influence of peers, mass media, and prevalent body image impact on eating patterns of adolescents.
- Personal self-esteem and body image guide the eating behaviour
- Missing meals and snacking(junking) are very common.
- Fast food centers are mainly patronized by adolescents – with soft drinks, burgers and pizzas being their favorite foods. These spoil the appetite for regular meals and are high in calories and low in nutrients.

Food selection is based mainly on availability, convenience, and time, rather than food value.

Signs of mild to moderate anaemia:

- Pale skin, including decreased pinkness of the lips, gums, lining of the eyelids, nail beds and palms.

- Dullness
- Easily get tired and exhausted
- Loss of concentration
- Getting breathless even on doing mild work.
- Increased heart rate.
- Restlessness.
- Instability.
- Sleepiness.
- Loss of appetite.
- Headache.
- Lack of interest in doing any work.

Signs of severe anaemia:

- Rapid heartbeat.
- Breathlessness even at rest.
- Gross tiredness
- Loss of hair.
- Edema of feet, hands and sometimes generalized oedema & Heart failure

What are the Consequences of anaemia in girls?

- Stunted growth.
- Weakness and tiredness.
- Lack of concentration.
- Poor school performance.
- Breathlessness.
- Miscarriage.
- Stillbirths.
- Low birth weight babies.
- Premature labour.
- Antepartum / Postpartum haemorrhage.
- Puerperal Sepsis.
- Higher risk of maternal mortality and morbidity.

How to prevent anaemia?

Eat foods high in iron

Red meat, Fish, Chicken, Eggs, Dried fruits, beans, and Green, leafy vegetables, like spinach and broccoli.

Observe cleanliness

- Washing hands with soap and water before and after passing motion and before eating any food prevents the passage of hookworm into the digestive tract.
- Wearing shoes while going out of the house and trimming the nails often, prevents the eggs of hookworm from entering the digestive tract.
- If there is excessive bleeding during the menstrual period, consult the doctor and take treatment, in addition to taking a more nutritious and iron-rich diet.

Dietary Advice

- Adolescents should be encouraged to eat a variety of foods from all the basic food groups, with plenty of gram products, vegetables and fruits, a moderate amount of sugars and salt and fewer fats, especially saturated fat.
- They should consume enough calcium, Iron and minerals to meet their growing requirements, and balance food with physical activity. The main emphasis is on the five major food groups, with a range of servings for each food group.
- Consumption depends on age and activity level. Teenage girls who are active, require about 2200 calories.

Eating and snacking pattern of Adolescents

Adolescents tend to eat differently than they did as children. Preoccupied with after-school activities and engagement in active social endeavors, adolescents are not always able to sit down for three meals a day. These apparent busy schedules may lead to meal skipping, snacking throughout the day, and eating away from home.

Many adolescents skip breakfast, but this meal is particularly important for getting enough energy to make it through the day, and it may even lead to better academic performance.

When adolescents skip meals at home is prevalent, the likelihood of purchasing fast food, which tends to be high in fat and sugar and provides little nutritional value.

Eating too many fast foods can lead to weight gain and may predispose one to diseases such as diabetes and heart disease.

Eating disorders:

Anorexia nervosa:

This condition involves eating less than required to maintain a lean body image. Although they are undernourished, anorexic adolescents consider themselves overweight and intentionally limit their intake of food because of a strong drive for thinness or fear of gaining weight.

The gross imbalance in nutrition with depressed estrogen levels may lead to:

- Lack of energy
- Stunted growth
- Poor bone health
- Slow heart rate
- Irregular menses
- Dizziness or fainting

Bulimia Nervosa: Individual eats large amounts of food and purge, trying to get rid of the extra calories. This may lead to:

- Life-threatening condition
- Severe malnutrition
- Depression

Avoidant restrictive food intake disorder- ARFID

ARFID is an eating disorder in which food intake is restricted and there is a general resistance to eating which results in significant nutritional deficiencies and extreme weight loss.

Those with ARFID avoid many foods because they fear choking or vomiting or they are disturbed by qualities such as textures, smells, or colours of certain foods ARFID Sensory factors Fear of Consequences Disgust Lack of Interest

Orthorexia Nervosa:

Obsession with "Healthy" eating is a type of disordered eating.

Eating disorders are not always about binge eating followed by purging or starving.

Having an unhealthy obsession with eating healthy is also an eating disorder. It is termed as Orthorexia Nervosa

Rumination disorder:

Rumination disorder involves the repeated regurgitation and rechewing of food after eating whereby

swallowed food is brought back up into the mouth voluntarily and is rechewed and swallowed or spat out.

Rumination disorder can occur in infancy, childhood, and adolescence or in adulthood

What are the complications of Malnutrition?

- Adolescents tend to take 40% of their calorie intake from these fat and sugar-rich foods such as soda, fruit drinks, pizza, burgers, and desserts. These foods can deplete the body's nutrition stores and increase the excretion of zinc and calcium.
- Poor nutrition leads to stunted growth, excessive weight, and obesity problems.
- Nutritional deficiency can manifest as psychological problems such as anxiety and depression.
- Intake of high sugar diet leads to dental caries, diabetes, and obesity in the future. They have altered lipid profiles and are likely to suffer from hypertension, heart disorders, and risk of stroke as adults.

- Malnourished adolescent girls tend to have pregnancy complications such as anaemia, abortions, intrauterine death of the baby, low birth weight babies, and preterm labour and lactation problems.
- Poor food habits increase the risk of oesophagal, stomach, and colorectal cancer.

How can we improve it?

- Though adolescents crave independence, they still look up to their parents. So it becomes the responsibility of the **parents to follow healthy eating habits**, which in turn the adolescent will follow.
- Make the adolescents involved in grocery shopping and planning the meal. This way they buy the food of their choice and will not complain about the available food.

Experiment with recipes:

- Instead of repeating the same dishes, present healthy food choices such as pulses, cereals, and vegetables in a more appealing way.
- Attempt different cuisine and prepare the meal according to the adolescent's taste preferences so that they enjoy having such food items.
- Follow regular meal times to avoid excess or unhealthy food intake. Teach children to eat only when they are hungry but not out of boredom. This habit cuts down unnecessary food intake.

Ensure to eat breakfast

- Eating breakfast regularly improves memory and concentration. Adolescents who eat breakfast regularly are healthier and have optimal body weight than those who don't.

- It is better to choose food rich in fiber, and low in fat and sugar for breakfast.

Snacks:

- Snacking is a common reason for junk food intake. Avoid buying foods you don't want the adolescent to have. Instead keep healthy snacks such as nutritive cookies, yogurt, nuts, fresh fruits, etc. available.
- Having meals as a family at least once a day, makes the parents aware of the food choices and habits of the adolescent which enables them to guide their adolescent in the right direction. In the present scenario of nuclear families and both parents working, ordering food seems easier and more affordable for parents and children.
- Instead of choosing junk food, if we make healthy food available, either by cooking at home or ordering from restaurants, adolescents start considering eating that food.

Eating out:

- While eating out, it becomes the responsibility of parents to make sure healthy choices are made without making the adolescent feel forced.
- Indulging oneself while eating out is reasonable if it is done occasionally.
- Now that eat out much more than before, it is important to watch what we eat.

Liquids:

- Plenty of water intake is a must to avoid dehydration.
- **Caffeine**, although a nervous system stimulant, is harmful if taken in increased amounts and may lead to sleep disturbances.

Restrict to one or two cups a day or choose a healthy alternative like herbal tea.

Dieting:

- Social media influence has made all adolescents body conscious. They do rigorous diets and exercises to avoid putting on excess weight which might lead to body shaming.
- It is necessary to help them to follow a healthy diet plan and improve their self-confidence. This can be done by a parent or teacher or counselor.
- Those who are worried about their weight, advise restricting calorie intake by reducing the quantity rather than stopping a particular group of food. Prefer non-processed food to avoid weight gain.

Avoid:

- Long hours of TV, digital games, or computers. Adolescents hooked to the TV or Internet, don't monitor what they eat, and how much they eat and stuff themselves with junk food which spoils their health.
- Restrict screen time 2 hours a day and engage them in physical activity. Making sure that our adolescents are not confined to their cots and rooms, improves their health and quality of life.
- Sedentary lifestyle. Activities with moderate intensity improve bone health, muscle mass, and strength. It also prevents chronic diseases in the future. It can be any activity like running, cycling, swimming, etc. These physical activities improve blood circulation, and oxygen supply and improve concentration.
- The basic suggestions include making fresh fruits and vegetables 50% of food intake, using whole grains, low-fat or fat-free milk, and varying food choices to keep it interesting.

- Adolescents are knowledgeable and exposed to information through schools and colleges. During this period we can correct deficiencies that occurred early in life and establish good dietary habits through various programs

Healthy food habits:

- Never skip meals or go for crash dieting.
- Have a proper breakfast and an early dinner.
- Limit fast food intake to a minimum.
- Have at least one fruit a day.
- Have salads often and vegetables daily

Avoid:
· Spicy and fried foods.
· No smoking and alcohol
Have:
· Regular physical activity.
What should I eat?

- Eating three regular meals a day with some snacks will help you meet your nutrition needs.
- Skipping meals means you will miss out on vitamins, minerals, and carbohydrates, which can leave you lacking energy or finding it hard to concentrate.

A guide to help you understand the value of what you eat.

1. Bread, grains, and cereals are carbohydrates that provide energy for your brain and muscles. They're also an excellent source of fiber and B vitamins. Without enough carbohydrates, you may feel tired and run down. Try to include some carbohydrates at each mealtime.
2. Fruit and vegetables have lots of vitamins and minerals which help boost your immune system and keep you from getting sick.

They're also very important for healthy skin and eyes. It's recommended you eat two servings of fruit and five serves of vegetables a day.

3. Meat, chicken, fish, eggs, nuts, and legumes (e.g. beans and lentils) are good sources of iron and protein. Iron is needed to make red blood cells, which carry oxygen around your body. If you are menstruating or have your period, this leads to a loss of iron.
4. If you don't get enough iron, you can develop anemia, a condition that can make you feel tired and light-headed and short of breath.
5. Protein is needed for growth and to keep your muscles healthy. Not eating enough protein when you are still growing, or going through puberty, can lead to delayed or stunted height and weight.
6. Include meat, chicken, fish or eggs in your diet at least twice a day. Fish is important for your brain, eyes and skin. Try to eat fish 2 to 3 times a week.
7. If you are vegetarian or vegan and do not eat meat, there are other ways to meet your iron needs, for example, with foods like baked beans, pulses, lentils, nuts and seeds.
8. Dairy foods like milk, cheese and yoghurt help to build bones and teeth and keep your heart, muscles and nerves working properly. You'll need three and a half serves of dairy food a day to meet your needs.
9. Eating too much fat and oil can result in you putting on weight. Try to use oils in small amounts for cooking or salad dressings. Other high-fat foods like chocolate, chips, cakes and fried foods can increase your weight without giving your body many nutrients.
10. Fluids are also an important part of your diet. Drink water to keep hydrated, so you won't feel so tired or thirsty. It can also help to prevent constipation. It is better not to drink flavoured waters or sports drinks because they can lead to more weight gainHealthy adolescents are the assets of a nation.

It is the collective responsibility of the nation, schools and colleges, and parents to properly

nourish and nurture adolescents with adequate vitamins and minerals to help them grow into healthy adults.

Educating and ensuring adolescents take a variety of foods from each food group along with physical activity will go a long way in bringing up

healthy adults.

"The most positive Ten Letter word is "CONFIDENCE," possess it!

CHAPTER SIX

Hygiene

From the Greek word **"hygies"** (hygiene-Goddess of health") - Meaning **"healthy."**

If good nutrition, Hygiene, exercise, rest, and suitable conditions for the specific needs of adolescents are available, many health problems can be prevented.

Prevention of disease strengthens the health of adolescents, and that of their family and the community they live in. Their future life will be better and easier.

Prevention of health problems is better than cure

For good health, having habits of cleanliness is essential.

Reasons:

1. The human body continuously accumulates waste products and dirt gets deposited over the body which needs to be removed.
2. The surroundings in which human beings live are full of pollutants, which need to be avoided to keep good health.

Health circle:

- Healthy communities help adolescents to be health
- Healthy adolescents can keep their families healthy. Healthy families can help the communities to be healthy
- Proper sanitation in the community, personal hygiene, cleanliness in the home and workplace, and protected water and

food, play a key role in preventing the transmission of many diseases.

- Individuals should take responsibility for personal hygiene as well as the cleanliness of their surroundings

Hygiene-different levels:

Personal hygiene:

Not following a standard of hygiene can have many implications.

Not only is there a risk of getting infections or illness, but there are many social and psychological aspects that can be affected.

What is personal hygiene?

It is the principle of maintaining cleanliness and grooming of the external body.

A regular routine of personal care

Washing and grooming of

- Hands
- Teeth
- Skin
- Hair
- Ears
- Nails and cuticles
- Feet
- Genitals

Hand hygiene or Hand washing:

- Clean your hands now and then by using alcohol-based hand sanitizers. This is because alcohol is a drying agent and kills all viruses and bacteria immediately.
- However, please note alcohol is liable to make your skin dry, thus always go for a branded alcohol-based fragrance-free hand sanitizer, which has a good amount of moisturizer in it.
- First, wet your hands and apply liquid or a clean bar of Soap.

- Next, rub your hands and scrub all surfaces (palms, fingers, and in between.)
- Continue scrubbing for 10-15 seconds. Soap combined with scrubbing removes germs.
- Rinse well and dry your hands

Teeth:

Healthy teeth and gums enable you to:

- Chew the food thoroughly
- Speak clearly
- Give shape and structure to your teeth

Structure of Teeth

Enamel(Top)The hard material on the outer surface of the teeth.

Dentin(Middle): Below the enamel- the bone-like material that surrounds the sensitive inner part of the teeth.

Pulp (inside): Tissue that contains blood vessels and nerve endings.

Dental problems

- Halitosis
- Tooth decay
- Plaque
- Tartar
- Periodontal disease

Causes

Infection: Dental problems are caused by the activity of certain types of bacteria in the oral cavity.

Other causes:

- Tongue not properly cleaned
- Food stuck in the teeth

- Sinus problems
- Stomach problems

How to avoid dental problems? Brushing and flossing:

- Brushing hygiene.
- Daily dental hygiene routine that consists of brushing teeth twice a day for at least 3-5 minutes.
- Make sure you do not put too much pressure as this can hurt your gums.
- Place the bristles along the gum line at a 45-degree angle. Gently brush the outer tooth surfaces of 2-3 teeth using a vibrating back-and-forth motion. Clean outer, inner, and biting surfaces of teeth with a scrubbing motion.
- Studies show an essential oil-based mouthwash reduces plaque by 70% and gum problems by 36% over brushing alone.
- Use an anti-microbial mouthwash to get complete protection from germs.

Floss your teeth:

Ease the floss gently between your teeth, and pull the floss smoothly back and front. Additionally, using dental floss will help remove food debris that's stuck in your teeth

Clean and brush the surface of your tongue daily because there are bacteria present particularly on the rougher top surface of the tongue.

These can contribute to **bad breath (halitosis)** and negatively affect your dental health.

Other precautions:

- If possible brush after every meal and rinse your mouth with warm water.
- Use a soft-bristled toothbrush.
- Replace your toothbrush after 2-3 months or after an illness.
- Use toothpaste that contains fluoride.

- Flossing removes food particles that are trapped between teeth and gum lines that rinsing and brushing miss.
- Eat at least 5 servings of fruits and vegetables each day.
- Include foods that contain calcium such as milk and yoghurt.
- Limit intake of sugar.
- See the dentist every 6 months

Skin

Skin is the outer covering of the body.

Layers of skin:

Epidermis: The outermost layer of the skin Cells of the epidermis make melanin

Dermis: The inner layer of the skin contains blood vessels, nerve endings, hair follicles, sweat glands and sebaceous glands.

Fat cells

Functions of the skin

- Protection
- Vitamin.D. synthesis
- Temperature control
- Sensation
- Water resistance
- Control of evaporation
- Excretion
- Absorption

Common skin problems

Bad odour

Perspiration itself doesn't smell. However, during sweating, another liquid, called apocrine is also secreted.

When the apocrine combines with the bacteria naturally present on the skin, odour results.

Causes:

- Poor hygiene

- Foods such as onions and Garlic

Acne

Acne appears when oil secreted by the oil glands mixes with the dead cells and plugs the hair follicles in the skin. It creates a white head.

Blackhead: When air touches the plug, the plug becomes black.

What makes acne worse?

- Oil-based make-up, sun tan oil, hair jells, and spray
- For girls, menstruation
- For boys, it may get worse because they have more skin oil
- Squeezing or picking at blemishes
- Hard scrubbing of the skin.

Management of Acne

- Daily baths or showering using soaps and Scrubbing the entire body with a Washcloth. Do not scrub violently.
- Wash the face two times a day with a mild soap or a gentle cleanser. It is best to use lotions if only needed.
- Use only oil-free and water-based.
- Use sunscreen every day during summer and winter.

Skin care tips

- Bathe or shower regularly using soap. Do not scrub violently.
- If possible, bathe or shower after exercise- especially after sweating.
- The use of antiperspirants decreases perspiration and covers odour with a manly smell.
- Wear clean clothes.
- Reduce stress levels that irritate the skin.
- Maintain a healthy diet.

- Wash your face 2 times a day.
- Avoid washing too often, as the skin becomes irritated and dries out.
- Keep your oily hair away from your skin.
- Avoid touching acne except when washing.
- Don't squeeze or pick the pimples.
- Try to avoid touching your face.
- Keep hands clean by washing them often.
- Protect yourself from the sun
- Apply sunscreen to the exposed parts of your skin when you go out.
- Wear a hat, tea shirt, and sunglasses.
- Drink plenty of fluids.
- Protect yourself from UV rays

Hair

- For many people, hair is a natural part of their looks and an expression of their personality. Hair can also offer protection: For instance, it helps to keep the sun's rays from reaching our scalp.
- Eyelashes and eyebrows keep dust, dirt, and sweat out of our eyes.
- Even the hairs in our noses and ears help to keep out germs and other foreign objects.
- Body hair helps to regulate our body temperature: The hairs stand up when it's cold,
- Keeping the air that is warmed by the body close to the body – like a warming layer of air.

What causes hair loss?

Because hairs continue to enter the resting phase and then fall out, we are constantly losing hair.

- A healthy adult may lose about 70 to 100 hairs on their head per day. But because new hairs are always growing and replacing them, this natural hair loss isn't noticeable.
- The rate of hair loss may increase noticeably if the hair roots are damaged during the growth phase or if a lot of hairs go into the resting phase at the same time. If no new hair grows and replaces the hair, that part of the skin becomes bald.
- This type of hair loss is referred to as alopecia – regardless of how large the bald spot is or whether it affects the scalp or body hair.
- In some types of alopecia, the hair may grow back. But baldness can also be permanent – one typical example is gradual hair loss in men (male pattern hair loss).

Hair care

- Wash hair regularly with shampoo. Rinse hair thoroughly with clear water after shampooing.
- Don't scrub or rub too hard. It may irritate your scalp or damage your hair.
- Massage your scalp well. It will remove dead cells, excessive oil, and dirt.
- Brush hair daily.
- Wash combs and brushes frequently.
- Don't share combs, brushes, etc.

Why brush your hair?

- Brushing helps keep the scalp by loosening and removing dust and dead cells
- It also adds shine to the hair.

Hair and scalp problems:

- Dandruff

- Head lice
- Splitting and breaking.

Dandruff

Dandruff is the Flaking of the outer layer of dead skin cells on the scalp. This condition is usually caused by dry skin. There is no cure for dandruff, but it can be controlled by special shampoos.

Head lice are parasitic insects that live on the hair shaft and cause itching. Lice can jump or fly from person to person, they are easy to catch from other people.

Avoiding and treating head lice.

- Don't share combs, brushes, hats, barrettes, or other hair things, headphones.
- Use special shampoo and wash your hair immediately.
- Any linen and clothes you have used should be washed in hot water or dry cleaned.

Splitting and breaking of hair

- Too much heat can cause the layered cells of the hair to split and even break.
- Wind, chlorine, chemical treatments, and permanent hair dye can weaken the hair in the same way
- If you put your hair in a ponytail, use a coated rubber band or soft cloth hair band
- Non-cushioned or uncovered elastic hair bands can cause severe breakage.

Ears

- Wash your ears with a washcloth. Don't forget to clean behind the ears

- Do not use Q tips in ears, it will smash ear wax deep into the ear canal
- Usually, ear wax is removed while chewing food or gum.

Nails and cuticles

- The part of the nail that can be seen and touched is composed of dead cells. The thin skin- like layer at the base of each nail is called the cuticle, a non-living band of tissue.

Nails

- Nails protect the sensitive tip of our fingers and toes
- Without proper care, they can become weak, ingrown or infected.

Nail Care

- Keep nails trimmed but do not cut nails shorter than skin level
- Keep nails clean
- Round your fingernails slightly when trimming them
- Cut toenails straight across
- Smooth rough nail edges with a file or emery board

Cuticles Care

- Clean and soften your hands in warm water
- To keep your cuticles neat, push them back after soaking your hands, while they are soft
- You may also use cuticle remover, a chemical that dissolves the cuticle.

Foot Care

- A large collection of sweat glands lives in our feet.
- Wash your feet well at least once a day.
- Wash your feet properly while having a bath, especially between the fingers.
- Dry them carefully, especially between the toes.
- Keep feet and skin clean and dry.
- Wear the right socks Change socks daily.
- Make sure your shoes aren't too tight.
- Wash the shoes or insoles of your shoes.
- Stay in bare feet at home.
- Avoid walking barefoot in public areas Bath
- Take Shower regularly.
- Showering helps get rid of dead skin cells, sweat, and dirt produced throughout the day.
- Use a gentle soap or bath gel.
- Washing your hair too often and with too much shampoo can dry your hair out, as shampoo gets rid of your hair's natural oils. Don't wash your hair every day, unless you need it.

Wear clean clothes.

- Keep in mind that clean underwear and clothes are a must! Do not wear clothes with stains, wrinkles, and smells on them.
- Sometimes reusing clothes are okay, as long as you are sure they're not dirty.

Genital hygiene:

- Protect your genitalia and prevent irritations and infections.
- It is very important to follow genital hygiene practices for both boys and girls.

Genital care for boys

- Wash your genitals with a finger. Shower on the outside normally.
- If you can retract the foreskin just rinse it in water and wipe it with a clean finger.

Genital care -Girls

- The vagina is a self-cleaning ecosystem of good bacteria, and your discharge (the clear fluid that comes from your vagina) is what sweeps out anything unwanted
- So Vagina is a self-cleaning organ, i.e. it cleans itself. But you need to clean the external genitalia using water and gently remove any possible dirt and debris.
- If you want to a cleanser, use only mild soap and avoid products with perfumes as they may irritate. Use only allergy-free and PH-balanced products.
- Use soft, white, unscented toilet paper and unscented feminine products.
- Don't use strong soap to clean your private parts, this will disturb your natural pH balance, and might result in yeast infection. It is good to clean any of the sweat and bacteria gathered around your inner thighs and your private genital area, but there is no need to clean the outer or especially inner parts of your vagina.
- Try to avoid tub baths as bath water is full of bacteria from the skin and these bacteria may reach the internal genital and urinary systems and cause infections. Instead, take showers.
- The genital region should not be wet, so avoid anything that causes dampness in the region. Dampness facilitates infections.
- So change your underwear soon after doing exercise and remove your swimming suit as soon as you are out of the water.
- The skin over the external genitalia will be very delicate. Avoid bleaching, waxing, and hair removers to remove hair

over the genital area.

How to fight Body Odour

- Keep your underarms and groin area clean and dry to discourage bacteria.
- Change out of sweaty clothes as soon as possible after exercising or perspiring.
- Trim or shave your underarm and pubic hair so there is less surface area allowing for the accumulation of sweat and bacteria.
- Cut back on alcohol and foods that may contribute to body odour, including curry, spicy food, onion, and garlic.

How to fight bad breath?

- Drink plenty of water.
- Brush and floss regularly.
- Treat any existing oral diseases.
- Eat crunchy fruits and vegetables.
- Cut out coffee.
- Chew sugarless gum.
- Eat yogurt.
- Take vitamins.

Cleanliness in the house:

- Wash the cooking utensils, plates, and glasses with soap and water. Dry them by keeping them in the sunlight. Sunlight kills the bacteria.
- All the rooms should be swept carefully. Dust under any articles on the floor should be removed by moving them and sweeping them.
- Walls and roofs should be cleaned now and then. Any cleavages in the walls or roof should be properly repaired to avoid any insects or animals lodging there.

- Keep the cots in the sunlight for some time every 15-20 days so that bed bugs and other insects will die. Remove dust from them.

  - Bed sheets should be washed often
  - Should not spit on the floor where people move around.
  - People with communicable diseases should be isolated.
  - Facility of a lavatory in every house is essential for the family members to keep in good health.

Sanitation in the community:

- Water resources should be within easy reach of the community. Animals should not be allowed to reach the water resource from where people fetch the water for their use.
- Build a fence around the water resource. People should not take baths and wash clothes near the water resource.
- People should not pass motion near the water resource. People should not throw the garbage where ever they like.
- They should keep the organic garbage in a pit in a corner of their yard to convert it as fertilizer or burn it so that it will not be invaded by flies, insects or animals which spread the disease.
- Water should not stagnate in the streets. Stagnated water is the best breeding place for insects and flies which spread diseases.
- If constructing personal latrines is not possible, at least community latrines should be constructed.
- Streets should be kept clean and bleaching powder should be sprinkled, where ever it is needed.

Protection of water:

- Drinking water should be fetched from a clean water source. If the water is dirty, keep the container static. The mud will settle down at the bottom of the container. Clear water above should be taken into another container straining with a cloth.

- Sunlight kills many bacteria. Keep the water in a glass container and keep it in sunlight from morning till evening.
- Boil water for about 10 minutes. Many of the bacteria will be killed.
- The container with the drinking water should be kept away from dust, animals and children.
- You should not immerse your hands in the drinking water container or glasses. You should take the water with a vessel having a long handle.
- While carrying water from far-off places, cover the container with a plate, otherwise dirt and leaves will fall into it and pollute.

Protection of food:

- Wash the vegetables before cutting.
- Wash your hands with soap and water before preparing and serving the food and also before eating.
- Cook the food properly. Half-cooked eatables may carry some diseases
- Cover the cooked food materials so that flies and dirt will not pollute them.
- Uncooked eatables like fruits or some vegetables, should be washed properly before eating.
- Eat the food when it is fresh. You should eat any food within 2 hours after cooking. If taken after 2 hours, you should heat it to the boiling point and then eat.
- You should not allow the animals to enter the kitchen.
- You should not sneeze, cough or spit near the food.
- You should not eat spoiled food. Changes in the smell, colour and taste indicate that the food is spoiled.

In conclusion Follow these hygienic practices:

- Brush the teeth in the morning and again at the night. Scrub the tongue.
- Daily bath with soap and clean water in the morning and evening. Underarms, groin and genitalia are to be particularly cleaned carefully.
- Take a head bath twice a week
- Remove the lice from the hair.
- Hands should be washed with soap and clean water - Before touching, cooking or eating food at any time. - after passing urine and motion - after attending and caring for a sick person.
- Washing eyes with cold water and cleaning nose and ears daily.
- Clean the mouth by gargling after eating anything, to avoid caries teeth and infection of gums.
- Remove footwear and wash the feet before entering the house.
- Wearing footwear before going out for passing motion.
- Trim the nails short.
- Avoid using others' combs, towels, toothbrushes, dresses, handkerchiefs etc.
- After passing urine and motion, genitalia should be washed from front to back, but not from back to front, to avoid the bacteria present in the anal region entering the vagina and urethra and causing infections.
- Cover the mouth and nose while coughing, sneezing and laughing.
- Pass urine soon after sexual intercourse to prevent urinary tract infections.
- Use only washed and clean undergarments. Better to use only cotton undergarments
- Cutting the vegetables after washing and cooking in clean utensils.
- Drinking filtered and boiled water.

- Eating fresh and properly cooked food and avoiding raw and half-cooked foods and food exposed to flies and dust.
- Covering the mouth and nose while coughing, sneezing and laughing to prevent droplet infection.
- Washing eyes with cold water and cleaning nose and ears daily
- Isolating a sick person with a communicable disease
- Sleeping under a mosquito net or using mosquito repellent

Make Hygiene a part of your daily routine

"Better keep yourself clean and bright; you are the window through which you must See the world" - George Bernard Shaw

CHAPTER SEVEN

Fitness And Exercise For Adolescent

Adolescents should be **physically active for good health**. If not, they put their current and future health at risk. Sadly adolescents worldwide are not sufficiently physically active.

Current global scenario

More than 80% of school-going adolescents globally did not meet current recommendations of at least one hour of physical activity per day – including 85% of girls and 78% of boys.

The global trends for adolescent insufficient physical activity show that urgent action is needed to increase physical activity levels in girls and boys aged 11 to 17 years. Reports indicate that girls were less active than boys.

The fact about living in modern times is that our lifestyles are less active than they once were.

Present lifestyles, like driving in cars or taking the bus, and even fun times, like watching movies and playing video games, don't require us to move.

We now know that how much you move is as important as what you eat to your overall health.

What is physical fitness?

A condition or state of being that helps you look, feel and do your best.

It is the ability to do tasks with full energy, and still be able to do other things with your time, such as schoolwork and activities with family and friends.

It is a basis for good health and well-being. Fitness involves the performance of the heart and lungs and the muscles of the body. Fitness can also influence how alert you are and how you feel emotionally.

Why does fitness matter?

Exercise is an important part of a lifetime of good health! Exercising is also fun and is something adolescents can do with friends. Regular exercise provides both mental and physical health benefits.

Exercise for Adolescents

Adolescence represents a critical period of development during which personal lifestyle choices and behavior patterns establish, including the choice to be physically active.

Encouraging healthy lifestyles in children and teens is important. Lifestyles that are learned in childhood are more likely to stay with the child into adulthood.

Some lifestyle changes can be harder to make as a person ages.

Promoting physical activity in early life is of the greatest importance to the healthy development of children and young people.

Exercise is an important part of keeping adolescents healthy.

Physical activity behaviors and health risk

Sedentary behaviour is an independent and important cause of chronic disease and contributes to one in six deaths in developed countries like the UK.

This bunch of behaviour, with the expenditure of very low energy, is highly prevalent in modern society.

Young adolescents spend an average of 6.1 hours each day watching television, using a computer or other smart technology, referred to as screen time.

A child born in 2013 will accumulate three years of screen time by age 18. Screen time is associated with obesity, CVD, and mortality.

Physiologically, a complex dynamic exists between the 'schedule' of regular physical activity, level of sedentariness, body mass index (BMI), fitness, and the link with non-communicable disease.

Insufficient physical activity is the fourth leading cause of global mortality.

Physical activity plays a key role in developing healthy cardiorespiratory fitness (CRF), which in turn correlates inversely with morbidity and mortality.

Physical inactivity, sedentary behaviour, and low cardiorespiratory fitness are strong risk factors for the development of chronic diseases with resulting morbidity and mortality, as well as an economic burden to wider society from health and social care provision, and reduced occupational productivity.

The process of cardiovascular disease (CVD) begins in childhood, and associated risk factors, including inactivity and obesity, begi n adolescence (ages 11–25 years)and continuen into adulthood, resulting in an enhanced risk of premature mortality.

Physical inactivity is a leading risk factor for ill health, going well beyond issues related to weight control and influencing physical and mental well-being.

Active overweight and obese people have around 50% lower non-communicable disease risk compared with unfit normal-weight counterparts.

However, within groups with similar fitness, the risk is higher for inactive individuals compared with those who follow physical activity guidelines.

The best way to promote healthy lifestyles is for the whole family to become involved.

Benefits from regular exercise or physical activity in brief:

According to the American Heart Association and the President's Council on Fitness, Sports, and Nutrition, the following are key benefits of physical activity:

- Improves blood circulation throughout the body.

- Keeps weight under control.
- Improves blood cholesterol levels.
- Prevents and manages high blood pressure.
- Prevents bone loss.
- Boosts energy level
- Releases tension
- Improves the ability to fall asleep quickly and sleep well
- Improves self-image
- Helps manage stress
- Fights anxiety and depression
- Increases enthusiasm and optimism
- Improved Metabolic health
- Increased musculoskeletal health
- Positive impact on cognitive development and socializing.
- Societal benefits by increasing social interaction and community engagement.

Risks of Physical Inactivity in brief:

- Overweight
- Obesity
- Diabetes
- Hypertension
- Cardiovascular diseases
- Abnormal cholesterol levels
- Various forms of cancer
- Impairment of concentration and productivity at school
- Social exclusion and loneliness.

The influencers of society, including national, city, and local leaders, religious leaders, celebrities in the glamour world, and the media, should promote the importance of physical activity for the health and well-being of all people, including adolescents.

Establishing an exercise plan A daily exercise program is a fun way to share physical activity with family and friends while helping to establish good heart-healthy habits.

Exercise guidelines for Adolescents

The following Exercise guidelines for adolescents can help them and their parent's plan activities:

- Adolescents need at least 60 minutes of moderate to vigorous physical activity on most days to maintain good health and fitness, and for healthy weight during growth.
- Physical activity should include aerobic, muscle-strengthening, and bone- strengthening exercises.
- Parents are encouraged to limit a teen's screen time (TV, video game, phone, tablet, and computer) to less than 2 hours daily and replace these sitting activities with activities that require more movement.
- Even low-to-moderate intensity activities for as little as 30 minutes a day can be helpful.

These activities may include the following:

- Pleasure walking
- Climbing stairs
- Dancing
- Home exercise

Impact of aerobic physical activity

- Regular aerobic physical activity increases an adolescent's capacity for exercise.
- It also plays a role in the prevention of heart disease and type 2 diabetes.
- Aerobic activities are continuous activities that cause the heart rate and breathing rate to increase.
- To prevent dehydration, encourage the adolescent to drink fluid regularly during physical activity.

- Also, have them drink several glasses of water or other fluid with no added sugar after the physical activity is completed.

Examples of vigorous activities:

- Brisk walking
- Running
- Swimming
- Cycling
- Roller skating
- Jumping rope
- Playing on the playground
- Dancing
- Gymnastics
- Hiking
- Soccer
- Tag games

The recommended **'schedule'** of Physical Activity(**PA**) in adolescents

Exercise schedule using FITT(Frequency, Intensity, Type and Time)

P/A Guidelines for young people aged **5-18 years**
Frequency-Daily

Intensity: Moderate to vigorous

Type: All P/A exercise and sports, muscle strengthening, and bone loading Exercises- 3 times a week.

Time: At least **60 minutes a day**. Minimise prolonged sedentary time.

Current scenario of Adolescents' physical activity:

- The proportion of active individuals declines significantly in adolescence, with girls less active than boys (56 vs 39%). This tallies with the continued rise in obesity rates among 11–15-year-olds, with 38% being overweight

- Increased self-consciousness and peer pressure through adolescence and puberty may be factors in declining PA involvement and therefore timely, sensitive engagement with this group is essential.
- WHO guidelines and the experience of member nations that followed these guidelines establish that children need to undertake at least 60 minutes of moderate-to-vigorous physical activity (MVPA) a day.
- Research has suggested that people should reduce extended periods of sedentary behavior, such as sitting at school or watching television, as these may constitute an independent risk factor for ill health regardless of other activity levels.
- Even highly active individuals are susceptible to the negative health effects of sedentary behavior.

Key strategies for Physical Activity Promotion Aims:

Incorporate small increments in daily routine

10 minutes of moderate and vigorous PA bouts are most beneficial to health, but light PA is more beneficial than none at all.

Active breaks at school and work to reduce uninterrupted sedentary behavior.

Stand up from sitting and stretch every 20-30 minutes.

Aims: Ascertain baseline activity levels and measure individual's internal changes

Remember that the capacity for PA naturally increases with maturation and growth.

Involve and educate to enable self-efficacy in PA management

Aims: Encourage family-based activity

Children of physically active parents are more active than children of physically inactive parents. Involve family in management.

Aims:

- Advocate active transport
- Promote PA as part of daily life

- Encourage walking part way to school or work
- Use cycle routes

Aims:

- Engage a wide range of stakeholders
- Support safe, sociable environments and green spaces
- Include schools, parents, and local authority
- Signpost to useful web-based PA information hubs such as local council or British Heart Association

Aims:

- Enable children to work together
- Establish schools or Physical activity hubs.
- Encourage links between adolescents, school, family, and community

Aims:

- Establish links to local services
- Be aware of local referral pathways

Priority policies in the strategy to improve physical activity in adolescents:

Adopt national guidelines tailored to the promotion of physical activity among adolescents.

Improve urban planning and transport infrastructure to promote active transport, such as walking and cycling to school.

Create environments to support physical activity for adolescents (such as free outdoor sport and leisure infrastructures, safe walking- and cycling-friendly routes, and clean beaches, parks, and forest areas).

Ensure school curricula for adolescents include a strong physical education component

Provide adolescents with opportunities for physical activity before, during, and after the formal school day.

Ensure adolescents with lower affluence or disabilities and those from minority ethnic groups have easy access to physical activity opportunities.

Benefits of regular physical exercise VS medical treatment:

Benefits of regular physical activity on health, longevity, and wellbeing 'easily surpass the effectiveness of any drugs or other medical treatment'

The process of cardiovascular disease (CVD) begins in childhood, and associated risk factors, including inactivity and obesity, track through adolescence (ages 11–25 years3) into adulthood, imparting a heightened risk of premature mortality.

Role of health care providers:

- Healthcare professionals caring for adolescents and young adults are ideally placed and suited to deliver powerful messages promoting physical activity and behaviour change.
- The healthcare professional is also ideally placed to engage adolescents in healthy lifestyle choices involving optimal PA to improve health and well-being.
- Healthcare professionals can also actively engage families, schools, and local authorities to support young people in an active environment.
- Every patient encounter is an opportunity to elicit PA and sedentary behaviour levels, and offer advice.
- This should be recorded within the social history, documenting daily minutes engaged in moderate and vigorous PA and time spent sedentary.
- Information and advice offered to the adolescent must be relatable in the context of their lifestyle and any coexistent medical conditions.
- They should advocate a PA 'prescription' for all young people within their healthcare plan. A useful tool for providing specific advice is the FITT principle.

- Every consultation represents an opportunity to ask about physical activity, Promote PA, provide advice, or signpost to appropriate pathways or opportunities.
- Key initial targets include getting everyone to reduce their sedentary behaviour and be more active, with even a little being more beneficial than none at all.
- Worrying trends in adverse physical activity behaviours necessitate urgent and concerted action.

Advice to Adolescents

- Stop telling excuses — make exercise benefit you
- Check out these exercise challenges and follow the solutions.
- I am too busy, and can't find time to exercise.
- It is something to do with making a priority. Fix a time that works best for you each day, like exercising after school. It's up to your choice to make the time and effort.

Exercise bores me.

Try different activities. Schedule different activities for different days of the week to keep things interesting. For example, you could swim on Sundays and do yoga on Thursdays.

Look at a list of fun activities like:

- Kickboxing
- Snowboarding
- Skateboarding
- Mountain biking
- Surfing
- Sandboarding
- Salsa dancing
- Kayaking
- SCUBA
- Pilates
- Yoga

- T'ai Chi
- Rock climbing

Remember that you will need permission from your parents/ guardian to invest time and money to buy safety equipment for most of these sports.

Also, remember that these activities carry risks for serious injury and it is important to learn the proper techniques before trying them out on your own.

Make sure to learn from certified teachers to stay safe.

Try them with expert guidance and supervision.

It's difficult to continue

Try exercising with a friend or a family member to give one another support. If someone else is counting on you to do the daily task, you'll be less likely to skip exercising.

I don't have equipment or access to a health club.

You can choose activities that don't require special equipment, such as jogging or walking.

Find resources within your community that are either low-cost or free, such as park and recreation programs. You can use your school's gym or swimming pool after school or on weekends. You could go for a long walk or easy jogging along with your pet dog.

Try jumping rope.

There are lots of ways to exercise that don't require a gym membership — be creative!

I don't know how.

Start with activities that you don't have to learn new skills for, such as walking, climbing stairs, or jogging.

Exercise with friends who are either beginners like you, or who are more experienced and can teach you what they know.

Take a class to learn new things, at your community centre or health club.

Once you get past these challenges, decide when you are going to exercise and which activities you would like to do.

What to wear to a workout Cloths

When you exercise, you should wear loose-fitting clothes that allow you to move freely. In the summer, wearing lighter colours will help you keep cooler.

Dark clothes, which trap light, will help keep you warmer in the winter. Wear layers when it is really cold.

It is good to wear hats or baseball caps for shade in sunny weather, and wool or ski caps in the winter to keep your head and body warm.

Never wear rubbery or plastic clothing because it won't allow your sweat to escape and your body can get too hot.

Shoes

Make sure your shoes are sturdy, fit well, and have heavy cushioned soles and arch supports. If you plan to run, getting shoes fitted by a sports shoe salesperson can be helpful. The wrong fit can be uncomfortable or even hurt you.

Socks

Socks help absorb sweat to help you avoid blisters. And, they might help keep your shoes from smelling bad!

Helmet:

Always remember to wear a helmet if you're doing a sport that needs one (like **snowboarding**, bike riding, or rollerblading).

Exercise, food, and fluids

Don't exercise with a full stomach. You may feel uncomfortable and your stomach might get upset if you exercise after eating.

Give a gap of 60 – 90 minutes for small meals to digest, and up to four hours for bigger meals or more or till you are hungry again. If you are competing in several athletic events in one day, such as a no. of tennis matches, eating small snacks in between events will help.

Water:

Water is the most important nutrient for your body when you exercise. Drink it before, during, and after exercise or sports competitions. You should keep drinking water throughout the next day after heavy exercise

Nutritional needs:

If you're playing sports, you have special nutritional needs. Adolescents who exercise need more food to support both their performance in their activity and growth.

You may need 2,000 to 5,000 total calories per day to meet your energy needs, depending on how active you are. But increased calories are only needed for those who play hard and for a long time.

Eating too many calories when you are doing light exercise could result in weight gain.

What happens if you do vigorous exercise and don't eat enough?

Your body may slow down. Your body may break down muscle instead of building muscle. You'll need to eat a good balance of vitamins, minerals, carbohydrates, protein and fats.

Feeling thirsty?

Feeling thirsty is not the first sign that your body needs water, as your body has already lost the fluids that you need.

If you have lost more fluids than you have taken in, that is called **dehydration.**

Signs of dehydration:

- A dry or sticky mouth
- Not being able to pass sufficient urine.
- Urine that looks dark
- Not being able to make tears
- Low blood pressure
- Rapid heart rate
- Feeling irritable
- Being disoriented
- Feeling dizzy or weak
- Having a headache

Correct dehydration If you are dehydrated, you need to replace fluids right away. Water is the best choice to prevent dehydration. If you feel faint and/or dizzy every time you stand up (even after a couple of hours), and if you have very little urine output, you should tell an adult and visit the doctor

Impact of Sports on girls:

The Women's Sports Foundation has researched the link between academic success and sports for women and girls.

Girls who participate in sports are less likely to fall prey to drugs, and less likely to involve in unhealthy sexual behaviour.

More likely to graduate from high school than those who do not play sports.

Half of all girls who participate in sports have higher- than-average levels of self-esteem and less depression.

80 per cent of women identified as key leaders in Fortune 500 companies participated in sports during their childhood.

Women who are student-athletes graduate at higher rates than women students generally.

Keeping safe and injury-free

- Things you need to do to stay safe and injury-free during exercise.
- Before you start exercising, you need to warm up your muscles. You can warm up by walking at an easy pace before stretching.
- Then stretch by starting at the top of your body and working your way down. Slowly stretch your calf, quad, groin, and hamstring muscles
- Warming up can also include jogging slowly, doing knee lifts, and doing arm circles.
- Make sure to cool down and stretch after exercising, too! A cool-down is a gentle exercise or stretch that helps the body return to its normal state after vigorous exercise.
- Cool-downs help your pulse (or heart rate) return to normal and can help prevent your muscles from feeling stiff after a workout.

Important exercise safety tips:

- Don't exercise when it is really hot and humid out. You do not want your body to overheat or get dehydrated.
- If it's very hot or humid outside, try moving your exercise indoors that day.
- If you live in an area with high air pollution, exercise early in the day or at night and avoid congested streets and rush hour traffic.
- Drink water before, during, and after exercise or sports competitions.
- Make sure you warm up and stretch your muscles for 5 minutes before and after workouts to make your muscles more flexible.
- It is easier to get hurt if your muscles are not stretched.
- It is also important to increase the intensity of your workout gradually.
- If you exercise intensely right away, you could risk getting hurt.

When to report to your parent/ Guardian or doctor?

- You are in severe pain
- You see swelling around where you got hurt,
- The pain gets in the way of sleep and activities.

Follow the precautions:

Don't jump back to your regular exercise after getting hurt because you could get hurt again.

Follow your doctor's orders for how to care for your injury and when you can be active again. including instructions for use of pain medicine.

Use the right safety equipment Helmets, Mouth guards, Special eye protection, the right footwear, Wrist, knee, and elbow pads

Female athlete triad

Some girls who play sports or exercise intensely are at risk for a problem called the female athlete triad. The female athlete triad is a combination of three conditions: disordered eating, amenorrhea (or missed periods), and osteoporosis. A female athlete can have one, two, or all three parts of the triad.

Eating disorders:

Most female athletes who develop an eating disorder are trying to lose weight so they can be better at their sport. This kind of eating disorder can range from avoiding certain types of food the athlete thinks are "bad" (such as foods containing fat) to serious eating disorders like **anorexia nervosa** or **bulimia nervosa**.

Menstrual dysfunction: A missed period is a concern for girls and women who over-exercise. Your body needs a certain amount of fat to function and to have regular periods.

Eating right and exercising are important for having a healthy body, but some girls take it too far.

Too much exercising or very strict dieting can use up your body fat and delay your period or cause it to stop until you gain some weight back.

Not having menstrual periods is called amenorrhea — a sign that hormone patterns have changed.

Oligomenorrhea is having very few periods, usually with cycles that last longer than 35 days.

Women who suffer from anorexia and elite women athletes who train seriously for competition often have amenorrhea or oligomenorrhea.

Low bone mineral density.

Osteopenia and osteoporosis are when your bones become weak. If a female athlete doesn't eat a balanced diet that includes plenty of calcium, she can develop osteopenia or osteoporosis.

This can ruin a female athlete's career because it may lead to stress fractures and other injuries.

Usually, the teen years are a time when girls should be building up their bone mass to their highest levels — called peak bone mass.

Not getting enough calcium during the teen years can also have a lasting effect on how strong a girl's bones are later in life.

"Physical fitness is not only one of the most important keys to a healthy body, it is the basis of

dynamic and creative intellectual activity."

"Exercise is King, Nutrition is Queen.

Put them together, You have got a Kingdom."

CHAPTER EIGHT

Conclusion

If Adolescents get clear information about various changes in Adolescence and puberty, dispelling the myths and misconceptions, about good nutrition and healthy eating habits, proper hygienic practices, and importance of regular exercise, they grow and develop to their maximum potential.

This book is a powerful tool to enhance the holistic positive health of Adolescents.

Preview Of The Next Book

Preview of the next book in the series, " adolescents - Reproductive Health Challenges"

The Female reproductive system: The female reproductive system includes:

- External genitalia
- Internal Genitalia
- Accessory reproductive organs

External Genitalia: The female external genitalia is made up of both the urinary tract and

reproductive structures.

Vulva, defined as covering or wrapping, includes both of these structures.

The vulva consists of the external female genitalia that surrounds the opening to the vagina:

- Mons Pubis
- Labia Majora
- Labia Minora
- Clitoris
- Urethra
- Vestibule
- External urethral meatus
- Hymen
- Vaginal orifice
- Bartholin's gland
- Skene's gland
- Vestibular bulb

All these organs are located in front of the anus and below the mons pubis:

Mons Pubis:

- Mons Pubis is located directly anterior to the pubic bones above the vagina and consists of adipose tissue. It gets covered with hair during puberty.
- This mound of tissue is prominent in females and it functions as a source of cushioning during sexual intercourse.
- The Mons pubis also contains sebaceous glands that secrete pheromones to induce sexual attraction.

Labia:

- Rich in nerve endings and blood vessels
- Protect internal genital organs against pathogens
- Function in sexual arousal

Labia Majora:

- The word "labia Majora" is defined as the larger lips. The labia Majora are a prominent pair of cutaneous skin-folds skin running from the Mons pubis to the anus and protecting the other external genital organs. They form the lateral longitudinal borders of the vulval clefts.
- The labia majora from the folds that cover the labia minora, clitoris, vulvar vestibule, vestibular bulbs, Bartholin's glands, Skene's glands, urethra, and the vaginal opening.
- The labia majora engorge with blood and appear edematous during sexual arousal. The outer sides of the labia are covered with pigmented skin and during puberty, hair appears on the labia majora. The inner sides are smooth and hairless.
- Beneath the skin layer, there is mostly fatty tissue with some ligaments, smooth muscle fibers, nerves, and blood and lymphatic vessels.

- The labia majora are comparable to the scrotum in males. They contain sweat and sebaceous glands, which produce lubricating secretions.
- The labia majora and the perineum are covered with skin similar to that on the rest of the body.
- The opening to the vagina is called the introitus. The vaginal opening is the entryway for the penis during sexual intercourse and the exit for blood during menstruation and for the baby during birth.

Labia Minora:

The labia minora or small lips are a pair of smaller cutaneous folds (fourchette) of skin that lie inside the labia majora and begin at the clitoris and extend downward and surround the openings to the vagina and urethra.

- Labia minora do not contain fat, hair follicles, or sweat glands.
- The folds contain connective tissues, numerous sebaceous glands, erectile muscle fibers, and numerous blood vessels and nerve endings.
- The skin is smooth, moist, and pink. A rich supply of blood vessels gives the labia minora a pink color. During sexual stimulation, these blood vessels become engorged with blood, causing the labia minora to swell and edematous and become more sensitive to stimulation.

Clitoris:

- The clitoris, located between the labia minora at the upper end, is a small protrusion that corresponds to the penis in the male.
- The clitoris, like the penis, is a sex organ in females that functions as a sensory organ and is very sensitive to sexual stimulation, and can become erect. Stimulating the clitoris can result in an orgasm.

- The body of the clitoris is suspended from the pubic bone by a short ligament and emerges to form a tiny external glans at the top of the vulva. Lying over the glans is a sheath of skin known as the clitoral hood.
- During sexual excitement, the corpora cavernosa and bulbs become engorged with blood, causing an erection.

Vestibule:
Vestibular bulbs

- The vestibular bulbs (homologous to the bulb of the penis in males) are structures formed from corpus spongiosum tissue. The vestibule bulbs are two bulbs of erectile tissue that start close to the inferior side of the body of the clitoris.
- The vestibular bulbs are believed to function closely with the clitoris. During sexual arousal, the vestibular bulbs will become engorged with blood. The engorgement of blood then exerts pressure onto the corpus cavernosum of the clitoris and the crus of the clitoris. This exertion of pressure onto the clitoris is believed to induce a pleasant sensation during sexual arousal.
- Below the urethral opening is the larger, vaginal orifice. The two Bartholin ducts open on each side of the vaginal orifice.
- Running along the sides of the vestibule are two elongated bodies of erectile tissue known as the bulb of the vestibule. Many mucous glands are also present in the vestibular region. Both the labia minora and labia majora tend to cover the vestibule.

The vestibule encloses

- Urethral opening
- Vaginal opening and Hymen
- Ducts from the greater vestibular glands

Urethral opening-External Urethral Meatus:

- Situated above the vaginal orifice, in the midline
- About 1 to 1.5 cm. below the pubic arch.
- The urethral opening is a small slit located closest to the clitoris; through this opening urine is excreted.

Bartholin's Glands:

- The Bartholin's glands also known as the greater vestibular glands (homologous to the bulbourethral glands in males) are two pea-sized glands located slightly lateral and posterior to the vagina opening.
- These two glands function to secrete a mucus-like substance into the vagina and within the borders of the labia minora.
- During sexual excitement, it secretes abundant alkaline mucus (a thick protein compound) which helps in lubrication.
- These glands frequently are sites of infection.

Skene's glands:

- The Skene's glands, which are also known as the lesser vestibular glands(homologous to the prostate glands in males), are two glands located on either side of the urethra.
- These glands are believed to secrete a substance to lubricate the urethra opening. This substance is also believed to act as an antimicrobial. This antimicrobial is used to prevent urinary tract infections.
- The function of Skene's gland is not fully understood but is believed to be the source of female ejaculation during sexual arousal.
- The glands are surrounded by tissue that swells with blood during sexual arousal and secretes fluid from openings near the urethra, particularly during orgasm.
- The two skene ducts lead from the skene's glands to the vulvar vestibule, to the left and right of the urethral opening, from

which they are structurally capable of secreting fluid that helps lubricate the urethral opening.

- Skene's glands produce milk-like fluid, secreted from these glands stimulated from inside the vagina

Vaginal orifice:

- Lies in the posterior end of the vestibule.
- It is completely enclosed by a septum of mucus membrane called a Hymen

Hymen:

- The hymen is located just inside the vaginal opening.
- The hymen is a thin piece of mucosal tissue that surrounds or partially covers the external vaginal opening.
- It's commonly seen as a small amount of extra tissue in a crescent-shaped or ring-like configuration around the edge of the vaginal opening.
- Hymen has no proven medical or physiological purpose.
- During puberty, estrogen causes the hymen to change in appearance and become very elastic.
- Normal variations of the post-pubertal hymen range from thin and stretchy to thick and somewhat rigid; or it may instead be completely absent.
- The hymen can rip or tear during first penetrative intercourse, which usually results in pain and, sometimes, mild temporary bleeding or spotting, but tearing or bleeding after first intercourse is not mandatory.

Is an intact hymen a sign of Virginity?

The state of the hymen is not a reliable indicator of virginity, although it continues to be considered so in certain cultures. The hymen can stretch or tear as a result of various behaviors.

- By the use of tampons or menstrual cups.
- Pelvic examinations with a speculum.
- Sexual intercourse
- Insertion of multiple fingers or items into the vagina, and Activities such as Gymnastics, Horseback riding, or Trauma caused by a "straddle injury."
- The most common myth around the hymen is that it remains “intact” until it’s broken during the first intercourse, which renders it a physical marker of virginity.
- Another common **myth** is that the hymen is **rigid and penetrable**. The tissue is actually stretchy and flexible, which means it does not necessarily tear with penetration.

Because of these factors, it’s impossible to tell by examining a woman if she’s a virgin

The idea that virginity can be measured or verified is perhaps the **most harmful and damaging myth.**

From puberty onwards, depending on estrogen and activity levels, the hymenal tissue may be thicker, and the opening is often fimbriated or erratically shaped.

In younger children, a torn hymen will typically heal very quickly. In adolescents, the hymenal opening can naturally extend, and variation in shape and appearance increases.

Misinformation and circulated myths about women’s health can be incredibly harmful to women.

Examination of hymen

- In cases of suspected rape or child sexual abuse, a detailed examination of the hymen may be performed, but the condition of the hymen alone is often inconclusive.
- For some women, there’s practically no tissue at all.
- For others, it’s a membrane covering the vaginal opening.

Imperforate hymen

An imperforate hymen is formed during fetal development An imperforate hymen occurs in 1-2 out of 1,000 infants.

It either completely prevents the passage of menstrual fluid or slows it significantly. In either case, surgical intervention may be needed to allow menstrual fluid to pass or intercourse to take place at all.

Complications

- If untreated or unrecognized before puberty, an imperforate hymen can lead to peritonitis or endometriosis due to retrograde bleeding.
- Additionally, it can lead to mucometrocolpos (dilatation of the vaginal canal and uterus due to mucous buildup) or hematometrocolpos (dilatation due to collection of menstrual fluid).
- Mucometrocolpos and hematocolpos can in turn cause urinary retention, constipation, and urinary tract infection

Diagnosis

- An imperforate hymen is most often diagnosed in adolescent girls after the age of menarche with otherwise normal development.
- In adolescent girls of menarcheal age, the typical presentation of the condition is **amenorrhea and cyclic pelvic pain, indicative of hematocolpos secondary to vaginal obstruction.**
- An imperforate hymen is usually visible on **vaginal inspection** as a bulging blue membrane.
- If hematocolpos is present, a mass is often palpable on **abdominal or rectal examination**.
- The diagnosis of an imperforate hymen is usually made based purely on the **physical exam**, although if necessary the diagnosis can be confirmed by **transabdominal, transperineal, or transrectal ultrasound.**

Management

Before surgical intervention in adolescents, symptoms can be relieved by the combined oral contraceptive pill taken continuously to suppress the menstrual cycle or NSAIDs to relieve pain.

Surgical treatment

Hymenotomy typically involves making cruciate incisions of the hymen, excising segments of the hymen from their bases, and draining the vaginal canal and uterus.

Hymenectomy can be done immediately after the neonatal period or delayed until puberty when estrogenization is complete.

Perineum: The area between the opening of the vagina and the anus, below the labia majora, is called the perineum. It varies in length from almost 1 to more than 2 inches.

Need A Small Favour

MAY I REQUEST YOU FOR A SMALL FAVOUR?

At the outset, a big **Thank you** for taking your valuable time to read this book. I highly appreciate your generous gesture of choosing my book among thousands of books that are published each and every day.

May I have few more seconds of your productive time?

I would love to have your precious review on my book. Reviews might not matter for big name writers, but they are of extreme help for new authors like me who don't have much following. They help me to build my readership with the readers. As the Reviews are the life line of any book, I request you to leave your review on the link below that will directly lead you to book review page.

Once again I extend my heart felt gratitude and await your exquisite review.

Please scan the below QR code to buy from Amazon:

Book Link:

About The Author

Dr. Vijayalakshmi Aluri is a writer of around **150 short stories,** authored **4 novels, and 4 health education books-"Matrutvam"**(Advices to the Pregnant women), **"The story of our body"**, **"Adolescent girls' health'"**- in regional language and **"Adolescents' Health and Behavior"** in English

Translator of world-famous health education books from English to Telugu:

"Where there is no doctor", "Where women have no doctor", and "Where there is no Psychiatrist" published by Hyderabad Book Trust and

"The story of blood", "Thumpa and sparrow" and "Tortoise wins again" were published by the National Book Trust of India.

1,00,000 copies of 'Adolescent girls' health' were distributed to high school, college, and out-of-school girls with the financial assistance extended by the Govt. and non Govt. organizations.

Her stories won prizes conducted by different Magazines.

Many of her stories and talks were broadcasted by All India Radio.

Participated in Poets' meet twice, organized by the most popular Television, Hyderabad.

Wrote a column for many years in **Vanitha**, a magazine for women, by Chandamama group of publications, with the title **"Health successes."**

Mrs. Sujatha, a research student, at Nagarjuna University, selected Dr. Aluri Vijayalakshmi's literature as her Thesis subject and got her degree.

Essay titled **"The impact of cinema on society,"** published by A.P. State Literary Academy was later included in the textbook of P.U.C., Banglore University

The essay, titled **"If a doctor is also a writer"** was included in the textbook of B.A., Open University, Hyderabad.

Her story, translated into English, **“Flower Garden”** was **one of the 12 best stories** among around 1500 stories translated from all Indian languages in a competition conducted by **“HUMANSCAPE”**, a fortnightly English magazine.

Dr.Vijayalakshmi Aluri’s name is included in **“Who is who of Indian writers”** and **“Who is Who of Indian Translators”** published by Central Literary Academy of India

Books By The Author

Book#1) The War:

A Collection Of Real Life Stories To Empower The Women To Face The Challenges, Be Resilient In Tough Situations, And To Emerge As Warriors '

The War' is a compilation of 7 stories projecting the different issues propelling the lives of people and providing insights into women's struggles to empower themselves in the present-day socio-cultural scenario. Women, anywhere in the world are subjected to disrespect, inequality, injustice, exploitation, endless abuse, gender discrimination, gender pay gap, gender violence etc., more so in India, a country where women are given the status of a goddess.

'The War' inspires the people to let their hearts be filled with empathy in the unprecedented calamities like the Covid pandemic. It reflects the plight of health care personnel working in the most vulnerable conditions, yet preserving the human feel. It mentions the existing inequalities exposed by Lockdown and inspires people to have humane relationships with others, especially in tough times.

'Flower Garden' emphasizes the importance of nurturing human values. The story declares that though money is the pivotal element in our lives, there are many vital components of human life that are more precious than money. It also affirms that no person should die because of the non-availability of healthcare at right time. (This story was selected as one of the best 12 stories out of around 1400 stories translated into English from almost all Indian languages, by Humanscape, a magazine from Mumbai)

'Break the shackles' represents the life of educated and earning women surrounded by the shackles of patriarchy and their struggles to overcome the hurdles. While men can enjoy both a secure family and a career, women face many visible and invisible roadblocks to having them. They would be threatened emotionally and culturally to opt for any one of them. It questions the patriarchal society which denies women the right to have autonomy and decision-making power.

'Quagmire' questions the systems which allow the mafia gangs to make the drugs as easily available as chocolates in colleges, schools, and universities, leading to the destruction of the future of the youth. Itcriticizes the apathy of the citizens and society at large when systems fail to control the evils of society. It also gives a lucid picture of the innocent youth drowning in the quagmire of addictions.

'The Path' shows a path to the present-day youth to become responsible and productive citizens of the country protecting themselves from becoming prey to the newly emerging vices in modern life..

'Burning furnace' gives a bird's eye view of the impact of globalization and its offshoot, new economic reforms encouraging special economic zones, huge big dams, etc, driving the common people away from their lands, their villages, and their livelihoods. It questions the unjust policies of the Governments, which should have an obligation to protect the people. The story also questions the development model in which the fruits of development do not trickle down to the poor and widens the gap between the powerful rich and the powerless poor.

'Fragrance' portrays the struggle of a resilient woman, who was forced to leave her village to escape from hunger, depression, and violence from her husband and toil in the city to bring up her children. After reading these stories, you will have a vivid picture of the sentiments, emotions, valor, perseverance, hopes, aspirations, and goals of people, especially women, apart from their struggles, sufferings, and sacrifices in a traditional socio-cultural setting.

All the stories have a common ideology,

"Humankind is my business"

Read, enjoy, and join this most beautiful business to transform this world happier

Book #2) BATTLEFIELD (A Compilation Of Real Life Stories To Inspire and Empower Women In Their Fight Against Gruelling

Situations With Valor And Triumph)

Are you fed up with reading mere imaginative and mock stories?

Are You Passionate About Have A Fresh Experience Of The Intense True Stories With Different Dimensions Of Life?

Do you want To read the stories of women who are victims of poverty and patriarchy?

Do you want to get inspired by the Empowered and Courageous women who stood up against all odds?

Then proceed To Read these real-life stories These poignant stories, from the pen of a compassionate doctor, hold a mirror to present-day society.

The stories deal with themes ranging from incest to the trials and tribulations faced by the voiceless underprivileged to the present-day horrifying situation the world is in, due to the epidemic, and particularly the alarming medical crisis our country is faced with.

Despite the horrifying circumstances which could plunge any person into the depths of despair, the resilience, tenacity and strength of character displayed by the protagonist of **"The Inferno"**, one of the stories, is no less than a beacon of light and an inspiration to the many unfortunate women.

Yet another story portrays the plight of the unlettered voiceless and disadvantaged people bringing to light the inequitable society we live in. The story, **"Battlefield"**, provides readers with a gallery view of the happenings occurring at a frenetic pace in a hospital. Furthermore, the practical problems faced by the Frontline workers, tasked with handling Covid cases, are shown from a human perspective.

Printed by Libri Plureos GmbH in Hamburg,
Germany